THE DOLPHINS AND ME

The Dolphins and Me

by DON C. REED

Illustrated by
Pamela and Walter Carroll

Sierra Club Books | Little, Brown and Company
SAN FRANCISCO | BOSTON·TORONTO·LONDON

To Ernestine, and all the dolphins,
who so enrich our lives.

The Sierra Club, founded in 1892 by John Muir, has devoted itself to the study and protection of the earth's scenic and ecological resources — mountains, wetlands, woodlands, wild shores and rivers, deserts and plains. The publishing program of the Sierra Club offers books to the public as a nonprofit educational service in the hope that they may enlarge the public's understanding of the Club's basic concerns. The Sierra Club has some sixty chapters in the United States and in Canada. For information about how you may participate in its programs to preserve wilderness and the quality of life, please address inquiries to Sierra Club, 730 Polk Street, San Francisco, CA 94109.

First Edition

Library of Congress Cataloging-in-Publication Data

Reed, Don C.
  The dolphins and me / by Don C. Reed.
    p. cm.
  The author, a former diver, describes his experiences with and observations of the dolphins whose underwater world he shared for more than thirteen years at California's Marine World / Africa USA.
  ISBN 0-316-73659-7
  1. Dolphins — Training — Juvenile literature.   2. Dolphins — Juvenile literature. [1. Dolphins.]   I. Title.
GV1831.D65R44   1989
636.08'88 — dc19   88-26526
                                                                   .CIP
HC   AC
10 9 8 7 6 5 4 3 2 1

Sierra Club Books/Little, Brown children's books are published by Little, Brown and Company (Inc.) in association with Sierra Club Books

Printed in the United States of America

Acknowledgments

How can I thank all the animals and people I've learned from? It's impossible to name more than a few. However, without park president Mike Demetrios's personal commitment to Marine World, the park would have gone under, and there would have been no dolphin stories for me to tell. I must of course thank Jim Mullen, Marine World's head dolphin trainer, for his friendship and his patience with my endless questions; likewise Sonny Allen, twenty-year veteran trainer and head of the entire marine-mammal training department. Inspirational and helpful in many ways were John Lilly and the late Antonietta Lilly, whose loss is mourned; Dr. Diana Reiss, head of Project Circe; senior trainer Debby Marren-Cooney and trainers Judy Peterson and John Lawrence; and Alan Therkelsen, Roberta Quist, John Racanelli, Gene Heck, and all the many divers who shared these adventures, each of whom deserves to have his or her own book (Keith Worcester, if you are still on the planet, please drop me a postcard in care of the publisher).

I would like to thank Earth Art Works director Steve King for the loan of many dolphin books, which were especially valuable for checking information on early dolphin oceanariums; Pamela and Walter Carroll, the artists who lent their hard work and talent to the illustrations for this book; copyeditor Peggy Freudenthal; Helen Sweetland, my editor at Sierra Club Books; and Fred Hill, my agent, the first person who took me seriously as a writer. Marine Mammal Fund director Stan Minasian and wildlife artist Lou Silva deserve awards for outstanding friendship and the wisdom of their conversation.

Finally, I want to send verbal hugs to my family, especially Jeannie, Roman, and Desirée Don, and Barbara and David and Dad; to Ken and the family Shiels; to my students at Horner Junior High School; and last, to the dolphins themselves.

Thank you, all, very much.

Contents

A Note to the Reader

Everything in this book really happened, but not always in the order in which I've described it. I worked as a professional scuba diver at Marine World/Africa USA for fourteen years and eleven months, and dolphin adventures from that entire underwater career are included in this book. In retelling them, however, I have jumped back and forth in time freely, fast-forwarding or rewinding the events.

In some cases, I have attributed the actions of one dolphin to another of that species who was also at the park. I did this because I have known approximately thirty dolphins, and even for the most dedicated reader, that is too many similar animals to keep track of. Accordingly, I have shortened the list to about half a dozen main characters.

All conversations in this book were reconstructed years after they happened and are doubtless inexact.

Finally, the section on the dolphin Gordo's life in the wild is necessarily fiction, as no human eye was there to see.

With the aforementioned exceptions, this story is true.

DON C. REED
Fremont, California
April 1988

1

My First Dive with the Dolphins

I stood on a narrow, red-painted stage above half a million gallons of cold salt water.

A wave slashed foam onto the stage and across my bare feet. I had a black rubber wetsuit on but neither a hood nor "booties," those heavy neoprene shoes that divers take for granted nowadays. It didn't occur to me to ask the other divers why we had neither foot nor head protection. I wore what the other folks wore. I wasn't about to complain: if the other divers had jumped off the edge in their underwear, I would have just shrugged and done the same.

That cold, windy March day in 1972 was my first day of work as a professional scuba diver for Marine World, soon to become Marine World/Africa USA, an oceanarium-zoo in Northern California. I didn't let on how strange everything felt. I was only six months out of deep-sea-diving school and had almost no idea of what to expect.

The hard rubber mouthpiece still felt foreign clenched between my teeth. It seemed clumsy to breathe through my mouth instead of my nose. Each breath had to be "asked for," pulled in by a conscious lifting of the chest, creating a vacuum to suck in the compressed air.

Not wanting to dangle my legs in the water, I stood awkwardly on one foot at a time as I fumbled into the big, floppy swimfins.

As I pulled the black plastic mask over my face, the strap tugged at my hair. When I opened my eyes, my field of vision was narrowed by the mask. It was like staring through a section of pipe.

I took one giant step forward and fell . . . into another world.

I heard the crash of the surface as it broke apart and thumped shut above me; I felt the massage of pressure and the cold water rushing down my neck and spine. Air bubbles slid ticklingly up my face, heading for the surface, while I headed the opposite way, falling, dragged down by the heavy lead work belt around my waist.

As the bubbles of my entry cleared, my vision returned. My fintips folded softly underneath me as I landed on the green, algae-covered floor.

Oddly, I didn't spot the dolphins right away. Perhaps their dark/light camouflage patterns broke up their outlines. Then, all at once, there they were — and so much *bigger* than I had expected. It's only the magnification down here, I told myself, a trick of underwater light. But I knew they weighed between 300 and 400 pounds each, as much as a giant professional wrestler or the biggest lineman on a football team.

I tried to remember the one-minute human-dolphin co-existence lesson that head diver Ted Pintarelli had given me.

"Spock — that's the one with the hole in his fin — he won't bother you. Neither will Delbert: he's got a shark scar on his belly that makes him easy to spot. The smallest one's Ernestine; she's okay. Lucky is king bull, the toughest dolphin in the tank. You'll recognize *him* right away: there's a purple spot on his cheek, and he's big, and all scarred up from fights, and . . . well, you'll know him!

"But Arnie, he's one who'll give you trouble. He thinks he's bad, and he likes to try and scare new guys in the tank. Like he might swim fast at you or something. Just hold still if he does. Don't let him chase you out of the tank or he'll make a game out of it, and you'll never get any work done. Don't look scared. He'll leave you alone . . . most of the time, anyway," the muscular, red-faced diver had added with a grin.

I had always thought of dolphins as sweet and gentle, like Flipper on the old TV show, who was sort of an ocean-going Lassie, man's best friend in the sea. Now I tried to figure out which one was Arnie. He was supposed to have a lower jaw shaped like a hook, whatever that meant. But it was no use: I couldn't tell the dolphins apart. They all looked like trouble to me.

As the streamlined but massive gray creatures cruised around me, I reminded myself they were not sharks. Their eighty-eight white, needlelike teeth, which I could see so clearly, were meant for snagging swift herring on the run, not for ripping out a twenty-pound mouthful of flesh, as a white shark's teeth were. Dolphins were mammals, not fish, and the reason for the up-and-down motion of their tails was to bring them back up to the air.

Some said dolphins were smart like people. Certainly dolphins could do things with sonar that we humans couldn't match. In one experiment I read about, dolphins were able to distinguish between two types of identical-looking plastic-coated wire — one with a lead core, the other with a copper core — just by sending their special clicking sounds inside them.

Well, I wasn't getting a whole lot of work done this way. In the distance I could see the three other divers, already lying down on the floor, their scrub brushes busy. As it was for them, cleaning algae off the underwater floors and walls and windows would be 95 percent of my job. The other 5 percent, the head diver had promised, would be magic.

None of the divers had air tanks. Each diver breathed through a thin yellow air hose leading up to the surface, where it was plugged into a brass outlet on an air compressor. I noticed the strange shape of the bubbles as they left my regulator and wobbled to the surface. They were not round but dome-shaped, flat on the bottom, and they changed as they rose toward the mirrorlike surface twenty feet above.

In my hand was a short, iron-handled scrub brush. I held it in the special way Ted had shown me.

"If you hold it the regular way, like a hairbrush, you can't get anything but wrist power behind it," Ted said. "But upside down, the bristles are next to your palm, and you get your whole body into it. Switch hands every ten or twelve brush strokes, too, so's you won't have to stop and rest."

Lying down in a sort of push-up position, I took an experimental scrub stroke at the floor. The brush was neither motorized nor self-operational. My tentative push did not accomplish much. Some scratches appeared in the green algae; that was all. The stuff clung like paint!

The algae has to be taken off, or it grows thicker and thicker and finally rots, breaking off at the roots, clouding the water, clogging the filtration system, and plugging up the windows. There are chemical ways to kill algae, of course, but these cannot be used because they are harmful to the dolphins' eyes.

So we divers scrubbed. Algae was our job security!

I turned the brush on edge, so that the stroke it made would be one inch wide instead of six, and leaned all my shoulder strength behind the stroke. Now the brush bit. There. I had a one-by-twelve-inch piece of clean white floor. Just eleven more strokes and I'd have one whole square foot finished. And since the tank was 60 by 80 feet, that meant there were only 4,799 more square feet to go.

Suddenly a blur of movement caught my eye. A dolphin was hurtling toward me. Although it was closing the distance between us unbelievably fast, I saw it as if it were in slow motion.

The dolphin's lower jaw hooked over its top one: it was Arnie. His head moved up and down violently, and his tail moved so fast that a trail of bubbles formed behind it. As the dolphin charged, I heard a roar of cavitation as the very water tore, breaking into hydrogen and oxygen.

I didn't even have time to flinch properly. It was easy to do just what Ted recommended. I froze.

I knew that if the dolphin ran into me at that speed, whatever he hit would be broken. This was how dolphins were able to kill sharks: they smashed their insides with a high-speed ram.

Whooosh! I felt rather than heard a wash of water like a great wind. I saw the dolphin's stomach — he had a belly button! — then the animal turned like a veering jet.

But not to go away. No more than six feet from me, he stopped. I saw his narrow face, saw his jaws move, heard the *klonk* that I knew signaled aggression. His white teeth gleamed, sharp and clean as if they had been brushed. But dolphins do not fight seriously with their teeth.

In a motion so fast my mind had to reconstruct it afterward, the gristly ridge on the underside of the dolphin's tailflukes suddenly appeared right before my face. It was as if a baseball bat had been swung at my head — and stopped an inch before my face caved in.

Again I did nothing, but not through courage. My reflexes are slow. I had time to tell myself, Hold still; don't do anything to make him think you want to fight. I also had time to feel a wave of anger at this huge animal for picking on me for no reason at all.

Then another dolphin, heavy-bodied with a purple spot on the left side of his beak, eased into my vision, and Arnie casually swam off with him.

When my heart and breathing rates returned to relative normality, I went back to my work. I scrubbed and watched, and watched and scrubbed. My shoulders began to feel pumped full of blood, as they do in weightlifting workouts.

Suddenly something shining caught my attention. I turned my head, and the whirring roar of the regulator seemed to disappear.

In stillness like the hush in a cathedral, I saw the smallest dolphin move her head just slightly, and from the back of her neck something silvery emerged, as if she were manufacturing a halo.

Naah. Yes! There it was: a glistening, gleaming, silver bubble ring, rising. The dolphin flexed her neck again, and another ring emerged, rising faster, so that it joined its luminous relation and they merged, becoming first a figure eight and then a larger single circle, a Hula-Hoop of light.

After I'd spent nearly two hours in the water, the scrubbed-off algae was rising in darkening clouds, like night closing in.

I kept switching the brush back and forth, from hand to hand, trying not to think about Arnie. Long ago, in India, there was a saying that you should not worry about tigers, lest you bring one to you by the thought.

Still, I couldn't help wondering where he was. My head began to shift back and forth more rapidly as I tried to see, but couldn't.

Just then, something touched me!

I rolled, ready to fight, and looked into the red-brown eye and the face of . . . who?

It was definitely not the hook jaw of Arnie, and the purple spot of Lucky's cheek was not there. Spock was supposed to have a hole in his left pec fin, while Delbert had a shark scar. This must be Ernestine.

I told myself she wasn't really smiling: that happy look was just an accident of jaw formation, indicating nothing more than lines of bone and muscle. But looking at her made me feel happy just the same.

She was so beautiful. From a distance, the dolphins had looked simple, uncomplicated. But up close, everything about Ernestine was astonishing. The black pupil in the center of her red-brown eye seemed to radiate emotion. Six inches back from the eye was a fold of skin with an opening the size of a pinhole in it, the opening to her ear. Even the dolphin's skin was special: not perfectly smooth, but textured with the tiniest of lines, and colored with subtle gray patterns that were perfectly matched and fitted together, like the interlocking feathers on a hawk.

She had pectoral (chest) fins to steer with, tailflukes for power, and a blowhole at the back of her head that could release breath at 200 miles per hour, punching a hole in the ocean spray so the dolphin could inhale relatively dry air and not drown in a storm. From the shape of her beak — the reason for the name "bottlenose" — to the elegant flare of her tailflukes, she was a creature of wonder. I felt I could study her for a thousand years and not see everything.

Ernestine nuzzled in beside me and laid her pectoral fin on my back.

This amazed me. A big animal I had never met before, and it swam up and touched me!

I couldn't resist her. Without conscious thought, my hand reached up and stroked her side. It felt smooth, soft, and firm, like the inside surface of a hardboiled egg.

Suddenly the dolphin rolled, bringing the fin on her back into my hand. Then she took off. The suddenness of the motion frightened me, and instantly I straightened my fingers, releasing the loose grip I had held so as not to make her feel restrained. Had I offended her?

But she turned and came back, rolling again to place her dorsal fin (the one on her back) in my right hand.

Why fight it, I thought, dropping my scrub brush.

This time, when Ernestine took off, I went along.

I left my human clumsiness behind. For glorious seconds I knew what it was to be the swiftest swimmer in the sea. She towed me, and I tried not to get in the way. I was conscious of my body's shape as an obstruction and tried to narrow myself.

We soared. The water rushed past my face and swirled around my body, and I felt the streaking lines of speed.

Klonk! At the sound, Ernestine flicked out and away from my hand and was gone in an instant. I hung in the water, becoming a sluggish human once again.

Before me "stood" a gray-white dolphin giant. There was no question as to his identity. I knew it was Lucky even before I saw the scars on his face and neck and shoulders, and the dark spot on the left side of his jaw.

The dominant dolphin lowered his head slowly. Again I heard the noise of irritation, threat, or challenge, and for an instant I thought he would give me trouble for getting too friendly with Ernestine. But the *klonk*ing sound was softer now, as if the point had already been made.

I was in the presence of a leader. Whether I labeled him "alpha male" or "dominant dolphin bull" or "king among his own kind" made no difference. This chunk of sea was Lucky's territory, and he was very definitely in charge.

There was depth to Lucky, and intelligence. It was an

intelligence different from my own, perhaps, but certainly deserving of respect. He looked like he knew how to live and how to die, like an Apache chieftain living in the wild, who would find hardship and danger at every turn and was content that it should be so.

I did not understand all this at once, of course. I had no words to express what I felt then. There were only raw emotions, ideas, possibilities. My brain felt staggered, like a computer with information overload.

Trying to show neither fear nor aggression (and certainly not disrespect!), I let myself drift down, settling slowly back to the floor of the tank, to my dropped scrub brush, to my work.

Lucky only watched me go, and made no move to follow.

2

The Dolphin Who
Challenged an Orca

≈≈≈

*I*t was half-past summer and a quarter to noon.

The other divers and I were just sitting down on the bench behind the dive shack. The morning's scrub was behind us, and I had just picked up the giant red-and-white plastic heavy-duty insulated lunchbox my wife Jeannie filled with goodies every morning.

With my thumb on the lunchbox button, I paused a second to savor the anticipation. I loved lunch anyway, and today there was something special inside.

I sighed and opened the lid, but I didn't see what I was looking for right away. I had to push aside a plastic bag full of tortillas rolled around peanut butter and blackberry jam before I spotted it. There! A round plastic container with a white square showing through the lid. It was a slab of my wife's best dessert: champagne cake with custard filling. It took eight eggs to make it, and the frosting slathered across the top was white and rich with sour cream.

"Food truck's here!" somebody yelled. I cursed silently at the driver's bad timing as I slid the lunchbox into the shade under the bench.

A big brown van was backing up to one end of a very long building with a corrugated metal roof. The door of the building was eight feet tall and had a handle as long as my arm. I grabbed it and leaned back.

There was a crack as ice broke away from the rubber insulation, and the door swung slowly open. Inside, in North Pole temperature, were cardboard boxes stacked on pallets.

Outside, the back of the truck was opened up, and divers and trainers and everybody else not desperately busy formed a human chain. One of the divers bounded up onto the truck and started tossing down boxes full of restaurant-quality fish: mackerel, smelt (both Columbia River and silver), squid, and herring. The boxes leaped from hand to hand as though they were alive.

"How much do they eat?" I asked sandy-haired old-pro trainer Jim Mullen as we worked side by side.

"Who?"

"The dolphins. I read where the head of some fishermen's union in Israel wants to kill dolphins because they eat three or four hundred pounds of fish a day."

"Who said that?" Grunt, lift, throw.

"Yaakov Friedler, head of the Israeli Fishermen's Union.

He says dolphins are the gangsters of the sea, and he wants to give them rat poison because they eat their bodyweight in fish every day."

"A big dolphin will eat maybe twenty pounds of food in a day."

"Not four hundred?"

"No."

"How much does Lucky eat?" I asked, naming the dominant dolphin.

Jim stopped, box in hand.

"Right now," he said, "Lucky isn't eating at all."

Lucky. The dolphin king. In the half-year I had been with the park, I had heard more stories about this overwhelming personality than about all the other dolphins put together. It was hard to know where the truth ended and the legends began. But after having known the animal even for a short time, I would have believed almost anything about him.

One story I heard had to do with a conflict between the dominant dolphin and one of his trainers.

For reasons of his own, Lucky had been refusing to perform, and one of the trainers had become so frustrated that he had picked up a light plastic pole and thrown it at Lucky, hitting him in the side. A diver had had to go in and get the pole afterward, which he did not enjoy, but Lucky did not harass the wetsuited human. No, according to the story, Lucky waited until the following day, when the short-tempered trainer was working on a ladder fixing the big jump hoop high above the surface of the pool. Then Lucky had taken a twenty-foot leap straight up and slammed the trainer in *his* side, very nearly dumping him into the water far below.

Like everyone else who had contact with the dolphin king, I soon had my own Lucky story to tell.

I had been scrubbing the floor of the dolphin tank as best I could, considering I was being used as a toy by five full-grown dolphins. Dolphins can make playtime out of practically anything available to them, and divers are no exception. There were three straining bodies on one side of me, and two happy gray players on the other side. I was spun around, rolled on my back, and occasionally argued over. I felt like a human hockey puck.

But abruptly, shove-around time stopped. The dolphins must have found something more interesting to do. At last, I thought; now I can get some work done. Ten strokes with the right arm, shift the brush, then ten with the left. The algae was a rich purple-brown that day, and it came off easily. Every brush stroke cut right to the bone-white floor, and I was really ripping off some yardage.

But on the bottom, every so often, were some sturdy metal disks called pop-off valves. When the tank was drained and dry, these dinner-plate-sized disks would release ground-water from underneath to prevent the pressure of it from cracking the tank floor.

Suddenly my left knee was slammed into the sharp edge of one of those pop-off valves. That knee had been slightly injured long before in the sport of Olympic-style weight-lifting, and it was sensitive.

Now it felt like my knee had exploded.

Without conscious thought, I pivoted and slammed my

right elbow hard into the face of the dolphin who had caused the pain.

I turned and saw that it was Lucky — and realized too late what I had done.

Lèse majesté is a phrase that means to strike a king, a crime for which the penalty was once torture to the death. I had just struck a king who was quite capable of fighting his own battles.

Lucky seemed to swell. He barked, and the sound was accompanied by an explosion of bubbles from the back of his neck.

I felt jelly-spined, unable to protect myself, like a sea lion after a killer whale has crunched it into helplessness and then given it to the young orcas to practice on.

But then a sweet gray shadow slipped between us. I recognized Ernestine.

"*Ee-ee-eeee!* " Ernestine screamed at Lucky in a rasping underwater shriek. She snapped her jaws and shook her open mouth violently from side to side. She was protecting me!

It was as if Lucky were a very tough human fighter and Ernestine was his wife, and she was asking him not to beat up somebody.

"Come on, sweetie, he isn't worth it," she seemed to say. "You know you can take him; let's go get some air."

Ernestine angled her body up toward the sunlit surface, twenty feet away. Lucky looked at her, and then at me. I held my breath. Then the dolphin king allowed himself to be led away.

But just before they reached the surface, Ernestine turned back and snapped her jaws at me as if to say, "I stuck up for you this one time, but don't you ever give my Lucky trouble again, do you understand me?"

Yes, ma'am, no problem, I promise, absolutely!

I thought about what I had heard. Lucky was now refusing to eat. Why?

Once before, Lucky had gone off his feed, but then it had been for the most romantic of reasons.

In the park's early years, before I joined the staff, the dolphins and killer whales had stayed in separate but adjoining tanks, with three smaller pens for sleeping. Each pen opened out through gates into the much larger central pool, which was used for shows and free-swimming in Oceana Theater.

Now, all the dolphins in the show at that time were male, so you can imagine how Lucky must have felt when the stretcher came down from the sky one day and the most beautiful female dolphin in the world slipped lightly into the water: Ernestine.

Lucky appeared to go mildly insane. He leaped and twisted, spinning like a corkscrew, then dived and leaped and flipped again. He raced so fast it seemed as if he would smash up against the wall, but he veered off sharply half a body length away from it, zipped back to her, and stopped abruptly, posturing, as if to say, "Did you notice how wonderful I am?"

Then Ernestine shot around the tank, and Lucky followed. Their paths intersected and they touched as they passed. Lucky leaped, and Ernestine altered her course to be where he was coming down. As he cut the water they took off together. Like twin shadows they raced; like fountains intertwining they leaped. He matched his strength and speed to hers. It was dolphin ballet, a dance of oceanic romance.

But the next morning, when it was time for the dolphins to go back to their pens and let the killer whales have a chance at the larger swimming area, the dolphin couple could not be bothered.

The trainers blew their whistles and smacked an offering of mackerel on the surface of the water in the waiting pen.

But love laughs at cold fish. Ernestine and Lucky were lost in their own private world.

The trainers and divers brought nets and tried to herd the two dolphins into their pen. But Lucky was wise in the ways of men and their nets, and he showed Ernestine what to do. Like a gentleman holding a door open for a lady, Lucky picked up the heavy leadline at the bottom of the net, and Ernestine scooted underneath. Net-smart Lucky could both lift the net and zip under it by himself, needing no one to open a door for him.

When the net was repositioned for a second attempt to shoo the dolphins into their pen, Lucky added a little variety to his new friend's education.

"You can also do it this way," his motions seemed to say as he leaped lightly over the top of the net, and Ernestine followed.

Someone came up with the idea that if all the divers and trainers who had wetsuits on jumped into the water at once, they might intimidate Lucky.

Seven wetsuited humans jumped into the water all at the same time. But in less than a minute, the divers and trainers were hauling themselves back up onto the stage, making undignified noises and clutching various portions of their anatomy.

Lucky certainly had not seemed intimidated. He had casually beaten up everybody, dealing out a thump or a tail-smack or two apiece — just enough to give each person a thorough helping of discomfort, but not enough to seriously hurt anyone.

But the dolphins really did have to go back into their pen. It wasn't fair for the killer whales to have no free-swimming time — not to mention the fact that the shows could not go on. The trainers and divers tried every trick they could think of, with no result except their own embarrassment.

Then, at last, somebody thought: What about Kianu? What about the killer whale?

Kianu was a huge female orca whose name means "big woman" in Aleut — and it fit, as she tipped the scales at 9,000 pounds. In the wild, killer whales eat dolphins as a regular part of their diet, but Kianu had been raised with a dolphin as her tankmate. She had her own food supply, and like the orcas who swim side by side with dolphins where the salmon run, she had no need to think of a dolphin as lunch.

But Lucky and Ernestine would not know this, the trainers figured. When the dolphins saw that giant animal come out, they would beg for the chance to go back to their pen.

So, with a creak and a scrape and a groan, the stainless-steel gate was hoisted up.

And from her pen, four and a half black-and-white tons of orca — the mightiest predator in the sea — came forth.

Kianu just wanted to stretch her cramped muscles. Her

small holding pen was fifty feet across and bigger than most other aquarium tanks in the world. But still, she needed the larger space of Oceana's main pool to more fully exert her strength.

The killer whale paid no attention to Ernestine and Lucky. She did not think of them as food, because she had never hunted or eaten a dolphin. And as a source of danger? The thought was laughable. As far as size went, the dolphins were to her as mice are to a cat.

Lucky's reaction was the last one imaginable. He took one look at the gigantic animal emerging — and got mad.

How dare this creature interrupt his romancing! Lucky snapped his jaws and nodded his head sharply. He was threatening an animal who could swallow a dolphin without even bothering to bite it in half!

Kianu paid no attention to the dolphin's noise and posturing. It was a pleasant day, and the warm sun was shining on her gigantic back. She began to cruise around the tank, no doubt expecting only to be left alone, when —

Lucky charged at her. He raced toward the giant orca at top speed. It was no bluff. At the last instant before he slammed into her, Lucky flipped over frontward in a sort of dolphin judo roll and slammed his tailflukes against Kianu's snout.

She was shocked. This had never happened before! She turned and fled, and observers were treated to the incredible sight of a killer whale being chased by a madly jaw-snapping dolphin.

But the chase did not last long. Suddenly Kianu thrust her tailflukes down and flashed her pec fins out, as if to say, "Wait a minute: *I* am the killer whale around here." The

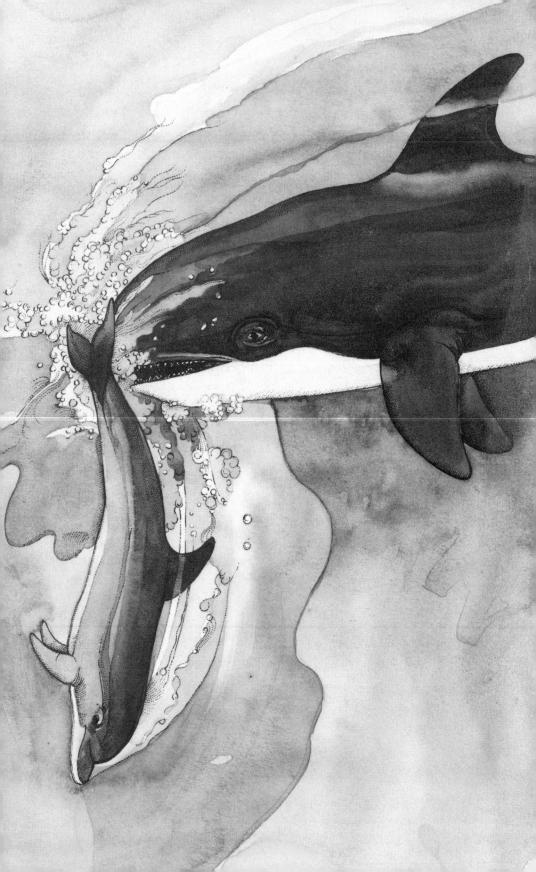

veins in the whites of her eyes engorged with blood, as a killer whale's eyes will do when it gets mad. Kianu turned around. And then she snapped *her* jaws, and the sound was like a safe door slamming.

Lucky, who was no fool, changed his mind and put on the brakes as Kianu charged.

Then was seen a demonstration of real dolphin speed. Around the pool a green wave rose as a raging, red-eyed killer whale tried very enthusiastically to catch up with one speedily departing male dolphin.

Lucky was very glad indeed when the trainers opened the gate to his pen just a little so he and Ernestine could slip quickly in, leaving an insulted Kianu complaining bitterly just outside.

"So what does that mean for us, that Lucky is not eating now?" I asked Ted Pintarelli later as I retrieved my lunchbox from the shade under the bench.

"If he won't start eating pretty quick, we'll have to catch him," said the head diver, crossing his ankles on the dive-shack porch railing.

"In deep water," he added, as if this were a thing of no consequence.

3
Dolphins on Strike

Ladeeez annnd gentlemen: Marine World puh-roudly presents . . . Dolphin Showcase Theater!"

On the red stage, trainers Jim Mullen and Jeff Pawloski both waved their arms as if they were throwing a fish. This was the signal for the dolphins' leaping "bow," and normally all five animals would explode from the surface of the pool.

But not today.

Today, when the trainers waved their arms, the dolphins just looked at Lucky. When he snapped his jaws, none of them moved.

The trainers repeated their command, but it was ignored. Lucky had put the dolphins on strike.

Jim and Jeff walked off the stage, while the announcer talked faster.

"Ladies and gentlemen, what you are seeing is a training technique called 'the burn' or 'time-out.' Imagine if you and I were having a conversation, and suddenly I turned and walked away from you. You would have a pretty good idea you had said or done something wrong, wouldn't you? That's how it works with dolphins, too. The time-out lets the dolphins know they're doing something the trainers don't want. Well, here are our trainers again."

Mullen lifted and dropped a small metal pipe set in a groove on the wall. This was a recall pipe, and dropping it made a noise underwater. To the dolphins, that noise meant, Come to the stage and you'll get a fish.

The dolphins did come over to the stage to receive the promised fish. Lucky allowed the others to eat. But when the gold-and-silver smelt reached him, he only mouthed it and let it go, watching the beautifully colored fish sink softly back and forth, side to side to side, down to the bottom twenty feet below.

Mullen, who knew exactly what was happening, called Lucky to the far side of the stage and tried to reward him first for following, and then for staying. Doing nothing is an important part of the show, because sometimes one dolphin does its own specialty and the others have to stand by and wait. But Lucky, though he had followed, would accept no food.

"Try Ernestine," said Mullen to Pawloski.

The younger trainer waved his arm in the fish-throwing motion.

Ernestine slipped underwater — but so did Lucky, and Ernestine bobbed right back up again.

Nothing doing. Lucky had said no.

"Try Delbert on the pec shake," said Mullen.

Jeff made a short flicking motion of his hand, the way Miami Dolphins quarterback Dan Marino would throw his bullet passes, beginning at the ear, rather than way back behind the head as most passers do.

The trainer had worked with Delbert, touching human hand to dolphin flipper and giving fish for the touch. Then the trainer had held his hand an inch or two away from the shark-scarred dolphin's pectoral fin. Delbert had waited for the touch, but when it did not come, the dolphin made contact himself, reaching up to the hand. For this he was rewarded heavily.

But now, nothing.

"Try Arnie on the vocals."

Pawloski wiggled his fingers hopefully, but Arnie didn't make his usual "aa-aa-aa-aa!" vocalization.

Mullen swore under his breath.

"As you can see, ladies and gentlemen, dolphins are free-spirited creatures!" said announcer Ron Mason.

And then Jeff Pawloski became a legend.

"I'll do the show myself!" the frustrated young trainer yelled to Mullen, and he dived into the water.

The audience was astonished. So was Mullen. So was the announcer. Even the dolphins were a little puzzled.

But there went Pawloski, diving down, "leaping" up in the bow the dolphins were supposed to do, then swimming to the stage to get his fish reward. Professional entertainers

both, Mullen and Mason instantly understood what Jeff was doing and went along with the slight change in the show, substituting man for dolphin.

While the announcer made jokes about people who love sushi, Pawloski ate the silver smelt reward in one quick gulp and then swam through the entire dolphin show. He did the Australian crawl through a hoop lowered into the water, retrieved tossed rings for the trainer, made a squeaking vocalization, wiggled his elbows for the "wave," and treaded water and offered his hand for the pec shake. He even turned upside down and thrashed both of his

wet-stockinged feet together the right number of times for the "arithmetic" joke, in which a person in the audience calls out two numbers and the dolphin supposedly adds them up and counts out the answer by lashing his tail that number of times on the water. How this is done should remain a secret, but the answer has nothing to do with mathematics and a great deal to do with how long the dolphin's head — or in this case, Pawloski's head — is underwater.

Finally Jeff "beached" himself, sliding on his belly up onto the stage, as the dolphins now would not.

The audience gave him a standing ovation, and Jeff Paw-loski's day as a dolphin would long be remembered.

But that sacrifice was hardly a substitute for a genuine dolphin show. Come to Marine World and see the per-forming trainer?

Still, the dolphin strike was at worst an embarrassing inconvenience. What was more important was that Lucky was still refusing food.

In time it became clear that the dominant dolphin would have to be taken out of the show and back to a smaller tank, where he would get medical attention and be force-fed, since he wouldn't eat on his own.

Lucky knows why we're here, I thought to myself in the water that morning: he knows what it means when there are nets, and divers without scrub brushes. We were there to catch somebody.

The dolphins watched us as we set up, as we anchored one end of the net then started to swim the other end across to the opposite side of the tank. Lucky swam off in one direction, and we followed him. He stopped for a second, hung motionless in the water, and then returned to his companions.

Arnie and Lucky had been fighting in the months before. In battles lasting as long as fifteen minutes, the combatants lined up some yards apart and charged at each other like knights on horseback, veering slightly at the last second, dealing out tremendous thunking blows of head and tail as they passed. Then they lined up to fight again.

Arnie apparently wanted to be king, because he kept attacking the dominant dolphin, acting aggressive toward the similarly sized adult male again and again. The fights always ended the same way: Lucky chased and Arnie fled, seeking to avoid a new set of scratch marks on his tail. Dolphins do not fight seriously with their small delicate teeth, but they will put marks on a rival.

But now, all differences seemed to be put aside. Like one animal the five dolphins swam, touching one another on all sides. As always, I couldn't stop myself from trying to guess what was going on inside their minds. What I thought was that Lucky knew we had come for him, and that he and they were saying good-bye.

The great dolphin separated himself from the others. Without looking back, he swam to where the divers were.

When we pulled the net between Lucky and the others, he made no move to rejoin them.

The net positioned, we put an extra weight belt here and there to hold it snug against the floor. We secured both ends and swam across the top of the net, into that quarter of the tank which now held Lucky.

There were three of us diving that day: Keith Worcester, Ted Pintarelli, and I. We wore our hookah lines, the yellow hoses leading to a surface air outlet. Our weight belts were stripped down; we needed to be able to move swiftly now. Ted was on the right, Keith took the left, I was in the middle.

Suddenly Lucky was before me. Like a statue of an ancient dolphin god he loomed, vertical, as though he stood. I saw the short stub of beak, the round spot of purple on his jaw, the smooth white chest and belly. His pecs were out, and he was inching slowly *toward* me.

I could hardly believe my good fortune. Here I was in

my first deep-water grab, and I was going to catch the dolphin king!

I balanced on my fintips, waited . . . and went for it, all the way, exploding forward with every ounce of speed and power I possessed.

I can't tell you how many times he hit me. That dolphin's head and tailflukes made me feel like an underwater punching bag. I forgot what I was in the water for.

When I remembered, there was a blue blur all around me and salt water in my throat.

My mask was knocked off my face. The regulator mouthpiece was missing from my lips. After half a moment's airless search, I located the dangling regulator and replaced it in my mouth. Then I fumbled around for my mask and finally found it on top of my head, the way an absent-minded professor finds his lost glasses in his hair. I snorted some air into the mask to clear the water out —

— and there was Lucky, hanging vertically in the water before me, exactly as he had a moment before.

The invitation was clear. "Would you like to try that again?" his body posture said.

No, I did not want to try that again. I would, I would try it again, because I had to, but definitely not because I wanted to.

Maybe I could kind of . . . sneak up on him? Turning my gaze away from him, pretending I was not interested, I casually edged sideways, pigeon-toed, across the white floor, coming five or six feet closer toward that old, sick, hunger-weakened dolphin.

I sneaked a peek to see how close I had gotten.

Lucky was the same distance away from me that he had

been before I started to move. He knew precisely how far a diver could leap from the floor before that first momentum died, to be replaced by the normal slow swimming speed of a human. The dolphin king was exactly that one lunge-length away from me.

Then Lucky flicked his tail and was instantly twenty feet in the distance. I wondered why the sudden respect, until the reason for it tapped me on the arm.

Oh. Hi, Ted.

Ted pointed to his own forearm, then to Lucky, and finally back to himself. Then Ted bit his own arm. After that he pointed to me and made a quick grabbing motion.

He wanted me to tackle Lucky while the dolphin was biting his arm? Well, okay.

I kicked after the diver's bubbles as he swam straight in at the sleek gray mammal, who was not noticeably nervous and did not seem inclined to run.

Holding up his forearm, Ted swam to the dolphin. Lucky seemed puzzled. What was he supposed to do with the forearm offered to him? Dolphins are not biters. They can make cat-scratch rake marks with their needle-sharp white teeth, but their mouths are built for snagging fish, not crushing bone.

But Lucky obligingly mouthed Ted's forearm anyway, and I made my move, lunging in from the side.

It almost worked, too. My arms encircled his rubbery back and chest. Four inches closer and I'd have had him wrapped. But close doesn't count, except in horseshoes, as the old saying goes. Lucky spit out what he was biting and rolled, twisting my arms and breaking my grip. Then *whack!* to Ted's head went that great dolphin's tail, and *whoof!* to my belly went the beak like a rock, and if he'd been human, I'd have said that Lucky laughed.

When the bubbles of that defeat cleared away, Ted kicked up topside for something. I watched his fins kick back and forth at the surface as he treaded water and talked to somebody on the stage. Then he dived back down and we tried some more.

As if we were the villains in a karate film, and the dolphin was the hero, Lucky made us look like fools. Nothing we tried worked for us. Did we lurk in the shallow underwater windows and jump out at the dolphin as he passed? Lucky swiveled casually and tail-slapped our faces for us.

But even in the midst of our embarrassment, what amazed me most was the restraint Lucky showed. He was holding back all the time. The dolphin could have broken us easily, snapped our bones, but he only hit hard enough to stop us for the moment. Like a boxer thumping an aggressive kid brother, Lucky was not trying for a knockout. Or a kill.

Ted, Keith, and I lined up at once and tried to corner him. Lucky disappeared with one kick of his flukes, vanishing like a gray ghost, only a swirl of water marking the spot where he had been.

Ted handed me a kinked-up snarl of our rubber hose, pantomimed me opening it and twisting it shut, and made a clamping motion with his arms. *What?* He repeated the gesture. Ted wanted me to try and lasso Lucky's tail with that length of kinked-up hose while he tackled the dolphin's upper half! Oh, no, Ted!

But Ted was Ted, and his eyes were bulging, and I would have given it a try if Lucky hadn't made the decision for us.

With easy strokes of his powerful flukes, the dolphin kicked to the surface and jumped the net, something he had not yet troubled himself to do. Maybe he wanted a breather, I don't know, but it meant we would have to reposition the net and —

Instead of the clean cut of his diving reentry, there was a froth of splashing confusion. Lucky was tangled . . . in the second net Ted had had set up.

"I knew he would jump sooner or later," said Pintarelli's rough voice when we had the net-wrapped dolphin halfway onto the stretcher. I didn't speak at all but only clutched my arms around that barrel of sleek muscle, desperate lest he explode in motion and we lose him again.

But Lucky made no move. He only waited, staring straight ahead, as if he understood that there was no chance of freeing himself. Not now.

But Lucky was still Lucky. He was the dolphin king.

And there were yet deeds to do.

4

The Showdown

We were force-feeding Lucky three times a day now. Morning, noon, and early evening we waded into the chest-deep water of the lowered holding tank and tried to catch the dominant dolphin. Once we had him, we had to twist wet towels around the ends of his jaws and carefully pull them apart. The rest of him also had to be controlled — held gently but absolutely still, so the delicate bones of his mouth would not be harmed by the force of his own struggle — while the vet stuck a Vaseline-slick hand and forearm right down the dolphin's throat, depositing herring, one by one, directly into the animal's stomach.

I knew it was for Lucky's own good, but I hated it.

He was looking particularly bad that day. He had been

throwing up the fish we gave him, and he was losing weight. The blubber on his sides was too thin, and his ribs showed through like curved pencils. He leaned to one side in the water, like an old grandfather who can only hear with one ear and so always keeps that ear turned in your direction.

I remembered how Lucky had been, the mightiest leaper in the dolphin show, so strong, a flier of the sea, overflowing with power. I felt my ribs want to shake, and my eyes clouded up.

Lucky cracked his tailflukes sharply across my shins and looked at me.

I managed to hold still, and part of me was proud of myself for how cool I was not to jump back in panic; but there was something else going on inside me, too — something deeper, a feeling both strange and familiar.

I remember when I was driving down a highway one night, and a coyote appeared suddenly in the lights of a freeway sign. Wanting to take a look, I had slowed until my car was barely moving.

Surprisingly close to the road, the small wolf-cousin squatted on its haunches, watching us, making no move to run away. I felt sorry for the little animal, living as it did on the edges of human civilization; always hunted, dodging guns, traps, poison; never knowing where its next meal would come from . . . and then I had one startling look directly into the animal's eyes. It was just my imagination, I'm sure, but clearly and sharply I felt this thought:

"Don't pity me. I am more free than you will ever be."

I went on, driving down the road in my planned direction. My schedule allowed no time for side trips. I had a job and a whole bunch of family and other responsibilities.

But the coyote trotted lightly in the direction that he chose.

I felt that same blaze of independence from Lucky.

Then he kicked me in the shins again, and I considered the benefits of the other side of the net. We caught him as a group that day, as I remember.

The vets had discovered that Lucky could keep down a mixture of chopped fish and cream, a foul-smelling predigested fish soup called "slurry." First we had to push a soft, clear plastic tube down the dolphin's throat, then a vet's assistant would raise the can of fish soup high and pour the white glop down the tube. The rest of us had to hold Lucky still. The process was slow and not fun for anybody, but it kept the animal alive.

It was especially awkward and painful for the vet's assistant, who had to keep his arm lifted straight up overhead while balancing the heavy can of liquid.

But one day we had a big truck crane available to us. Why not take advantage of it? We could hoist the dolphin right out of the water and work with him on dry land. We could put a soft mat underneath him, and the vet's assistant could just stand and hold that food can without straining his arm. It would be perfect, much easier for everybody, we figured.

The crane was positioned by the side of the tank, and Lucky allowed himself to be caught.

Gently we placed him in the stretcher, which was made of heavy-duty canvas folded over at each side to allow the insertion of two long and thick iron poles for lifting it.

A rope drew both ends of the stretcher poles snugly together over the top of the animal. The rope was then tied. Only the dorsal fin and the blowhole on the back of Lucky's neck now showed from above. His tailflukes stuck out from the back. All the rest of him was covered by canvas and the tied-together stretcher poles. Escape artist Harry Houdini would have had trouble breaking out from that.

There was a grinding *rrrrrr* and the crane hoisted, up, up — and stopped. The motor just quit.

The stretcher swung there quietly, halfway up the concrete wall. Rivulets of clear seawater poured from it, then the salty liquid dwindled to a drip, drip, drip.

"Come on with that motor!"

"Hurry up, get him out; he won't take too much of this!"

"I'm trying, I'm trying. Do you think —"

"Lower him down!"

"Let's go up and pull him out by hand!"

Ted was off duty that day, and everybody had a different idea. We all got very nervous . . .

Except Lucky, who calmly reared halfway up out of the stretcher. Were poles in the way? He bent them aside with a surge of muscle. Propping his pec fins on the stretcher poles, as if resting on his elbows, Lucky surveyed the situation below.

The crane started up again.

The dolphin dived for the water below.

But he couldn't reach it; his tail was caught. The canvas stretcher was still tied around his flukes! For an instant the dolphin hung suspended. Then he exploded into motion.

Like an out-of-control propeller, the dolphin flung himself in circles, whirling, changing directions at incredible speed.

There was nothing we could do. It would have been death to approach him then. That rock-hard beak would have smashed a human head like an egg hit by a hammer.

It would have meant death for the dolphin, too, if he hit the wall. He was just an inch or two from the concrete and hurtling so fast we could hardly see him. Yet even in frenzy he was a self-guided missile, and he did not touch the wall.

Then all of a sudden Lucky was loose in the water again. It was not possible: the dolphin had been firmly secured, the notch just in front of his tail had been caught between tied-together stretcher poles; he could not have broken free. Yet, somehow, there he was, swimming calmly, as if nothing had happened.

Behind him on the wall hung what was left of the practically brand-new stretcher. It did not look new anymore. The canvas was ripped and ragged, the material shoved to one end. The iron poles were bent and twisted, like wreckage from a fire.

"I think we better not catch him anymore right now," said the vet. "We don't want to overstress him."

To which there was no disagreement.

What Lucky was to dolphins, Ted Pintarelli was to dolphin catchers: the toughest individual I have known.

Like the dolphins, the head diver was so casual and graceful that at first he seemed smaller than his actual six feet and two hundred pounds. His physique was superb. When he leaned back, relaxed, with his wetsuit jacket off, his muscles lay in fine flat lines; when he stretched they ridged and knotted; and when he moved it was with the all-at-once explosion of an athlete or an animal.

Like the dolphins, Ted sounded intimidating when described, but what you felt when you met him was different:
you felt welcome, like being near a warm stove on a cold
winter's day. Ted's face was red, his eyes were large and
brown, and his voice was a friendly rasp.

When Ted smiled, which was most of the time, it was
with teeth that were not his own, except by right of pur-
chase. The originals had been kicked out by a horse and
their replacements shattered by a killer whale.

I don't know who the horse was, but the killer whale's
name was Ramu. Not Namu or Shamu (those are other
whales), but Ramu. He was resting at our park on his way
to Australia.

"We was force-feeding him," remembered Ted, "and I
guess he got excited, 'cause his tail twitched and the tip of
it caught me in the teeth." He drummed his thick fingers
on the desk.

"I like to think it was an accident," he said, " 'cause if
he'd done it a-purpose, he'd of killed me, easy."

In his private life Ted was a practicing modern-day cowboy, for real. He had a little ranch in the coastal hills where
he raised cattle. He broke wild horses to ride and wrestled
steers in weekend rodeos.

Once I'd watched Ted wrestle, on the asphalt behind the
dive shack.

There was a new diver, named Sydney, a farmboy from
Iowa or someplace, and Syd was hard. Broad-shouldered,
with square-cut biceps that crowded the elbow, and a couple
years' wrestling experience behind him, the new guy was
heavier than Ted, and naturally he wanted to take the head
diver on.

For a moment the two prowled around, studying each other's balance. The new guy looked stronger. But I saw Ted's face, and he looked happy.

Then Syd went into action. At first it was as if you had tossed two wild beasts into a pit: everything happened too fast to follow. But gradually a pattern emerged. The big blond guy would move swiftly, and stop, move swiftly, and stop. Fastfastfast — nothing. Then I could see what was happening. Ted was playing. He wanted to see every trick the new guy had. Syd would throw a half-nelson or a grape-vine hold at him, and Ted would seem to listen, as if he were thinking, Uh-huh, uh-huh, is that it? Then he'd break the hold or combination of holds, and wait for Syd to try something else.

When it became apparent that the new guy had shown all his moves, Ted got bored. He folded Syd up, knees to chest, as if he were a large package, and pinned him smack down on the pavement.

As a catcher of dolphins, Ted was the best. He got in tune with each animal's mood and followed it, varying his tactics according to the dolphin's experience and ability. As I had seen in the struggle with Lucky, if one move would not work, Ted would just try something else, improvising and improvising until something won for him.

He wouldn't give up. As killer-whale trainer Dave Worcester put it, "You can't stop Ted. Not permanently. He gets knocked down maybe, but he'll get up and keep coming. He's like Vince Lombardi, the coach of the Green Bay Packers football team in their best years. Lombardi said he never lost a football game, but he had the clock run out on him a few times, meaning if the game had gone on longer, he'd have found a way. That's how Ted is: once he has the job to do, he's not real big on backing off."

I was not present for the last confrontation between Lucky and Ted. If memory serves, I was in the hospital having a nose job: not for looks, but so that I could continue diving.

Inside everybody's nose is a little piece of gristle called the septum. In some people this septum gets bent a little bit to one side, half blocking the passage between nose and ears. This makes it hard to clear your ears, either automatically or by pinching the nose and blowing gently. Divers have to adjust to the increasing pressure of the water against their eardrums as they swim down. If a person dives too deeply without clearing, his eardrums will rupture from the weight of the water.

The operation was a minor one (though it swelled my face green and blue as if I had lost a fight), but it did keep me out of work for a couple of weeks.

So I missed the last meeting of Lucky and Ted. But I have the following account from half a dozen eyewitnesses, and there is no question as to its authenticity.

Lucky the dominant dolphin had not been struggling much anymore.

We didn't know it then (it seemed impossible that anything could really hurt him), but the dolphin's liver was barely functioning. He got tired, but rest did not bring his strength back. His body could no longer completely rid itself of toxins.

He was not getting better; his endurance, energy, and strength were nearly gone.

On the day that Ted and another diver climbed down the ladder to catch Lucky, the dolphin turned and snapped his jaws at them — twice, so there'd be no misunderstanding. He did not wish to be disturbed. "Leave me alone" was what his body posture said.

The head diver knew the dolphin was not bluffing. When Lucky snapped his jaws, it was for real. But not catching the dolphin would have been like abandoning him, denying him needed food and medicine. Lucky just had to be caught.

And then Ted looked at the diver beside him and hesitated. Band-Aid was the diver's name.

I don't know how he earned the name, but it fit. Band-Aid was thin to the point of fragility; he looked like if he sneezed too hard he might break something. He had guts and always did his share, and he was one of us. But willing or not, Band-Aid was just too light to be much help in a serious dolphin catch. Ted was afraid the guy might get busted up if things went wrong.

He didn't want to hurt Band-Aid's feelings, so he made a joke out of it.

"I'll catch this little dolphin by myself!" he said in a cartoon-macho deep bass voice, and everybody laughed, shouting, "Ride 'em, cowboy! Yee-haaa!" and similar encouragements, and Band-Aid obligingly moved back.

Then the laughter stopped as the diver pulled himself across the narrowing net.

Instantly Lucky was on him, flashing through the chest-deep water, ramming with his rock-hard beak.

Ted made himself into a ball, protecting his head and belly behind his forearms and raised knees, deflecting the dolphin like a spear off a shield.

The dolphin turned around and snapped his jaws once more.

Ted should have crawled back across the net. He could have sent for more help, or at the very least waited till later, when maybe Lucky would have calmed down and cooperated voluntarily.

But there was something else involved: that argument which is between the wild horse and the wild-horse breaker. Ted had once tried to break a stallion at night, and the horse had flung him off. But the head diver had gotten up, grinning in the moonlight, and in the morning he was riding.

No, the great disagreement was in the open now and would be settled. This time there was nothing and no one to intervene: no second-net trickery to entangle the dolphin, no teammates to get in the way; just the man who wrestled steers and the dolphin who had once attacked a killer whale.

Lucky dived, and Ted went after.

The bystanders saw bubbles and confusion as the combatants came together.

"He weren't too hard to find," said Ted of the incident later, "rammin' and pokin' like he was, and me trying to block him with my elbows, waiting for an opening. I saw my chance and got a hold on him. He slung me off.

"I ran out of air, and I guess he did too, because he came up right beside me. He breathed, and the air smelled bad, like he was dying inside. I went for him, the last time.

"Then Lucky threw himself forward, flipping over quick. His tail came across real hard. I brought my arm up to block."

The bystanders saw what looked like a harmless wave of

white water rise, and fall, across the diver's upraised forearm. Then the water was quiet.

Using his left hand, Ted pulled himself across the white floats on the net.

"I think my arm is broke," he said, shaking the water out of his eyes.

Other than that he made no complaint, and at the hospital the doctor did not take him seriously at first, especially since Ted would not let anyone scissor off the wetsuit sleeve.

"Wetsuits cost money," said Ted, grinning at the pretty nurse, though his face went white as paper when the snug wetsuit jacket was pulled off.

When the doctor came back with the X rays, though, his expression was considerably altered.

"A *dolphin* did this?" he asked incredulously. "Looks more like someone tied your arm to a steel table and then took a sledgehammer to it."

Both the major bones of the forearm were shattered. It took several operations, two heavy iron plates, twelve pins like wood screws, and a year in various plaster casts to heal the arm. There was so much metal in it that it dragged on Ted's arm when he went pleasure diving. In winter the metal got cold and the muscle surrounding it ached. Eventually he had to have another operation, to remove the iron plates and pins. Ted retained a zipperlike scar along one muscular forearm where the doctors had had to open it like a hamburger bun.

Back at the park, killer-whale trainer Dave Worcester was called away from a show. He phoned his brother Keith, home on his day off, and the two went in for Lucky, who after all this still had to be medicated and force-fed.

"You can imagine how we felt going after him then," said Keith. "But Lucky just gave up to us."

A few days later, the dolphin king lifted his head as if at the sound of approaching footsteps. He flung off those who were holding him and leaped and fell back, shaking, convulsing, then still.

He died as he had lived: unaided, unconquered, indomitable to the last.

For Ted Pintarelli, it was also an ending. He quit professional diving and retired to his ranch in the foothills, where he lives to this day: buying calves and selling steers.

He came back to the park once, though, to visit, and when we were sitting alone in the dive shack, just talking and remembering, I had to ask him a question.

Did he, well, did he *like* Lucky?

"Like him?" said Ted, as if the question were somehow improper. His red face pulled back and his eyelids squinched together as he struggled to put his feelings into words. "Course I liked him. Lucky was a good ol' boy. An' tough. He whupped me, and him sick at the time."

Ted frowned, not satisfied.

"I respected him," said Lucky's great antagonist.

Ted Pintarelli leaned back in his chair, crossing well-worn cowboy boots on what was now my desk. We talked for a little while about the continuing hassles in the dolphin tank, where Arnie was now in total control, with Lucky gone. At last the former head diver grinned and raised his fist, as if he held a glass to make a toast.

"He was number one," said Ted Pintarelli in tribute to the dolphin king.

5

Heirs Apparent

When Alexander the Great lay dying, all his generals gathered around him, each one wondering if he would be chosen to inherit the vast fortunes of land and treasure that the young Alexander had conquered.

At last one bearded leader could contain himself no longer. He leaned close to the dying boy king and tensely whispered:

"Alexander — to whom goes the kingdom?"

And Alexander of Macedon smiled and said, "To the strongest. . . ."

When Lucky died and Ted Pintarelli retired, there were actually three vacancies created, for Lucky had filled two spots. He had been first a leader and second a magnificent show animal. Last, of course, a new head diver had to be named.

The human problem was the least difficult. When Ted left, the diver who had been there second-longest took over. But he did not stay long, moving on after a couple of months, as did the person who followed him — and one morning, I found myself head diver.

My job did not change greatly. I still scrubbed floors and fed fish. The only real differences were a tiny increase in pay and the responsibility of making sure the work got done.

But the leadership change in the dolphin tank was not so easy.

The first thing Arnie did when we came into what was now "his" tank was to swim over beside each diver and hit us hard one time apiece. Then he made the rounds again, handing out a second helping of thumps. And then a third. And a fourth.

I told myself this was only temporary. It was natural to expect problems after a great leader died. There would be fighting among the dolphins to settle who would be in charge, and some of that was bound to spill over on us. Things would calm down.

But after Arnie had beaten up all the other dolphins a few times, so you would think the matter was settled, he turned again to the people in his pool. The trainers he couldn't reach, but we divers were in perfect range, and we had neither show training to distract him nor fish to bribe him with. He just kept after us.

The rough treatment did not quit. Tensions began to build. How could we live with this?

Every time we went into the tank that miserable summer, we knew we were going to get some trouble from Arnie. Some days he would travel in a circular path, going from one diver to the next, giving each one a casual knock on the head, a whack in the face, or a thud in the side. It got to the point where we could almost — but not quite — predict when it was our turn to get whomped. Arnie might keep this up the whole two hours we were scrubbing, pausing only if he wished to take a bit of a rest. Or, he might hit only two or three times during the scrub; we never knew.

We tried everything we could think of to discourage him. Maybe if we stayed close to each other, he would be intimidated? Naah. Huddling up just meant the dolphin had less distance to swim between handing out thumps.

Would he be less aggressive if we offered to play as soon as we went into the tank? We tried this, and it did work for a while, until Arnie got bored with play and came after us again.

Could the trainers help? One trainer stood by on the stage and rewarded Arnie for not beating us up. This worked as long as the food held out. But we couldn't expect a trainer to stand by and overfeed the dolphin three hours a day, two or three times a week.

Nets? Put a wall of knots between us and them as we scrubbed? That could be disaster. We had all heard horror stories of dolphins in other parks getting tangled and drowned in pieces of rope that had fallen into the tank at night. We weren't even going to try using nets.

Toys . . . now that was a possibility. We carried volleyballs and plastic garbage cans into the tank with us, and as long as the novelty lasted, we scrubbed in peace. But dolphins get bored easily. A quiet half-hour or so, and then, *bonk!* we would rub our heads and know the newness of the object had worn off.

I even invented a dolphin toy, a sort of Hula-Hoop made from black fire hose. I filled it with sand and metal scrap, weighting it so that it would neither float nor sink but only hang in the water where you left it. This would be perfect, I figured. It could be tossed back and forth, swum through, dragged around. If I were a dolphin I would lie awake nights dreaming about such a toy!

I put it in the water — and the dolphins were terrified of it. They would not go near my present. Hmmph.

Well, maybe we could use that fear to our advantage, I thought, and carried the hoop tucked under one arm while I scrubbed. This worked for about two blissful hours. Then Arnie gave the hoop a contemptuous nudge with his hook-shaped beak and went back to business as usual.

As the summer's heat climbed, so did the aggression.

Finally I got so frustrated that I went and whispered a few embarrassed words to Al, the welder.

He built me an aluminum anti-dolphin cage on wheels. The idea was that a diver would get inside the cage, which had no bottom, scrub the square of floor underneath, and move the cage ahead. Al's work came out beautifully, and it would have worked — but management found out about it and said no.

Almost the worst part of the problem was that people didn't want to believe us. A dolphin hitting divers? Incredible. Folks generally know four things about dolphins: that they swim in front of ships, fight sharks, have big brains, and never ever ever hurt people, no matter what, under any circumstances.

When I tried to say, hey, dolphins are wonderful, but there are exceptions to every rule, and some dolphins get very rowdy sometimes, my audience would look at me sideways, as though I were describing a savage attack by a bed of roses. I tried to explain that almost every life form has some way to defend itself — even roses have thorns — but it did no good.

At last I decided to do what another dolphin would do in that situation. The next time Arnie came over and rapped me on top of the skull, I put down my brush and stood up. Arnie hung in the water next to my face and looked at me as if to say, "Well, what are you going to do about it?"

Then he hit me again, square on the cheekbone.

I hit him back, twice, just as quick as I could, and I tried for three. Whonk-whonk-miss — left hook, right hook, missed with the last left because he wasn't there anymore. Two good hits right on that sharp-hooked beak of his, and for a second I felt wonderful. I reared up on my fintips and told myself that I had won.

But as I dropped back down to push-up position to resume my underwater janitoring, I caught a glimpse of something moving very fast.

Arnie hurtled across the pool, coming as if to smash something.

I flung myself over onto my back, with my knees and forearms up, like a cat on its back against a dog.

Arnie shot by me and instantly veered around, coming in from my blind side.

Spinning on my back, rotating on the biggest lead weight of my belt, I managed to keep facing him. With hands and flippered feet, I was able to deflect or fend off his blows, and I suffered no real injury. But even so, he thumped me around pretty well and appeared to be enjoying himself immensely.

I began to really hate Arnie. Why was he being so mean? I could see no reason for him to act this way. What had we ever done to him?

There was also the matter of filling the vacancy at top-deck. Who would replace Lucky as a featured player in the dolphin show? The answer to that question was presently swimming free, 300 miles south of San Diego, in that portion of the world ocean known as the Sea of Cortez. . . .

On a beach at the northern end of the Sea of Cortez, a group of white-clad fishermen talked and laughed and smoked cigarettes as they waited for the stars to fade.

At last one of the fishermen looked up at the sky and nodded. He said something to another man squatting in the circle of humans. The other laughed, and they rose and walked to the quiet surf. The second man flicked a glowing cigarette end into the foam, where its red light was extinguished with an audible *sssp*. The first man, not approving of such waste, stubbed out his cigarette on the unfeeling callus of his net-toughened hand and stowed the butt in his shirt pocket.

With neither haste nor hesitation, the two men waded into the shallow water. It was warm, and there was almost no difference in temperature between the predawn air and the comfortable sea.

Anchored in the waist-deep water just beyond the line of surf was a boat; its stern looked heavy, seemingly overloaded with heaping mounds of net.

In a moment, a key was turned. The racing sounds of ignition were heard, and then the sputter and catch of the internal-combustion engine.

As the boat motor started, the voices on the beach fell silent.

Five hundred yards away, a young male dolphin of the species *tursiops gilli* (pronounced GIL-ee or GIL-eye) lifted his head from the water. The dolphin humans would one day call Gordo looked very much like the more familiar Atlantic bottlenose dolphin (*tursiops truncatus*), only bigger. At 500 pounds, the Pacific dolphin was already larger at the age of three than most Atlantics ever get, and the full-grown dominant bull of the small tribe, or pod, weighed nearly twice as much as he.

Gordo's vision was not wonderful in air: a sort of jelly across his large, expressive eyes let him see both in water and out; but in dryness he could not detect details well. To him the boat was a large, blurry object with something like seaweed leaking slowly off its stern.

Lowering his head, the dolphin used his sonar along the boat bottom, bouncing several series of clicks off the ship's hull, listening to the echoes. The dots of returning sound added up to a picture in his mind. The mental image was of something that had not been dangerous nor edible before; he saw no reason to take interest now.

His mother did not seem worried either. At the sound of the boat motor starting, she had wakened, checking out the change in the environment, but only briefly. She had seen boats before.

The mother snuggled beside Gordo, touching him, reassuring him with her warmth and nearness, as dolphins do.

She stroked her pectoral flipper along her son's strong back. Gordo leaned his side against her in a sort of dolphin hug. Neither could know it would be for the last time.

The mother slipped instantly back into sleep, like the other members of the pod. There were six of them: the old "bull" and "cow" (the original New England whalers had first been farmers, and accordingly they called whales and dolphins by farming names), one young female, and three juvenile males, of whom Gordo was the oldest.

As the boat swung wide and slowly around the pod of dolphins, Gordo closed his eyes again.

Perhaps he dreamed. Certainly he had much to think about, for his young life was filled with adventure.

His natural home, the Sea of Cortez, was the most varied neighborhood in all the world ocean. The hills of land continued underwater — mountain ranges and sea-mount peaks with their tips broken off by some long-forgotten cataclysm; there were also deep canyons underwater, and currents winding like great rivers in the sea. Each environment had its own animals, and when the various creatures met, they hunted and feasted, and the survivors remembered and returned — to hunt and be hunted again.

What life! It has been said, "Anything that swims, you will find in the Sea of Cortez." This is an exaggeration, but not an unforgivable one, for there are creatures here in every imaginable size, from the largest thing that ever lived, the blue whale, which is as big as a swimming skyscraper, to the tiny green possum shrimp, which would look lost in the palm of your hand.

There are fish that grunt and are so named, and hammer-head sharks so swift and maneuverable they can turn back-flips in pursuit of their prey, and swordfish tough enough to fight and kill the sharks themselves. There are gray-green groupers as big as sports cars, and smaller ones of brilliant orange; huge and hurtling blue-backed tuna, and anchovy like shimmering light; brown manta rays as wide as class-rooms, leaping from the surface of the sea to crash back in thunder; and noctiluca, that microscopic plankton which is the ocean's nightlight, glowing blue-white when touched, so a child's hand could write her name upon the sea, and a swimming dolphin becomes a meteor.

Gordo had bodysurfed on the wave made by a whale; he had swum through storms, and survived; he had seen the ocean's visibility blocked by millions of mating ten-armed squid; he had hunted on the surface when the light gleamed like diamonds on the waves.

The family of dolphins owned . . . nothing; but could any palace match the grandeur of the jewel in which they lived?

But quite suddenly, Gordo's whole life changed.

Something like seaweed brushed against him. He moved away from it. It followed. The net was all around the pod of dolphins. The boat had completed its circle and was now back at the shore, where eager hands hauled in the long ropes that made a framework for the nets.

All the dolphins were instantly and completely awake

now, as each with sonar buzz or shriek tried to understand the clutching thing that was around them. Something was desperately wrong. This was not like anything they had experienced. Nothing they knew could help them now.

They tried to do what they had done with a similar problem in the past, when long arms of seaweed stroked them. They knew what to do for that: just hold still and let the weed float by, or very slowly swim away — slowly, slowly, that was important, lest the seaweed tangle and knot and drown them.

But what worked with seaweed could not work here. If they had leaped, they could have escaped. But dolphins do not leap over seaweed, and they did not know what to do in this strange and threatening situation.

The net was a wall of knots, and it seemed the only way to avoid its hurtful touch was to go in, toward the shallows. They did not want to go there, but the nets tugged them, and the crisscrossed knots made thin slashes like paper cuts on their delicate hides. In, in, the net forced them, pulling them to the shallows and the dryness and the sand.

Around Gordo now were tangles of netting and noise, bare legs and foam, and careful-stepping human feet. And then a long and heavy board was slid beneath his body, and four men lifted, making noises about the heaviness.

Their discomfort was nothing compared to what Gordo endured. For the first time he felt the full tug of gravity and the crush of his own weight. In the water he weighed slightly more than nothing; now, in an instant he had gained 500 pounds. Imagine how that weight felt, squashing down.

The dolphins barely resisted, seeming to have given up. They were in shock, that near-unconsciousness Nature gives to animals about to be eaten so they won't truly feel the pain of their own deaths.

In the shallows the dolphin mother watched uncomprehendingly as Gordo and his two brothers were carried out of the surf and placed on wet blankets on the back of a truck. The fishermen took the three youngest dolphins, since they were the most likely to survive the long trip. They would have taken the little female too, but by happy accident she had blundered over the floats and was loose.

The ancient truck started up. In fright and curiosity Gordo reared up, lifting his head to see. His widely opened eyes beheld what seemed to be moving land and the gleam of dawn on the sea behind him.

He saw the blurred shape of his mother for the last time, there where she waited, in the shallows of the Sea of Cortez.

Then a fisherman threw something dark and coarse and wet over his head.

The trip was a nightmare. This was in the last days before the passage of the Marine Mammal Protection Act, and the people caring for Gordo now were basically amateurs.

There were no soft, fleece-lined stretchers for the dolphins to lie on, nor zinc-oxide creams to protect their delicate skin from drying out. The humans didn't know they should turn marine mammals over from one side to the other. A dolphin's hide is not built for gravity, not meant to take the pressure of its owner's weight, hour after hour. Unless a dolphin is turned every half hour or so, its skin will chafe and crack and bruise, like terrible bedsores.

The fishermen were not cruel. They were just trying to feed their families the best way they knew how. They made a living by selling fish, and Gordo was a fish to them, something to be sold — the way a farmer would take cabbages to market.

They had no way of knowing how to take proper care of a dolphin. All they had were blankets, and some water in buckets, and the truck.

I was not there when Gordo arrived at Marine World, but I have talked to a trainer who was present at the arrival of a dolphin who was caught and transported under similar conditions. He said the animal's skin was so raw and chafed from not having been turned that the arrival pool turned pink with blood.

Gordo arrived at Marine World at about midnight. The driver had stopped at other oceanariums on the way, and now at last all the dolphins were sold.

A man with something shining around his neck drew in his breath with a hissing noise when he got a good look at Gordo's skin. The vet poked and prodded and stuck sharp things into the dolphin, but after his long journey, Gordo didn't care about such small things as vitamin injections.

Healing white zinc-oxide cream was soothed onto the dolphin's skin.

At last Gordo was lifted and set on the edge of a small training tank.

He heard a rippling sound below him. Water.

"Wait till he breathes!" somebody yelled, but Gordo had no time for this.

The dolphin lunged from the wall, and the water's cool embrace soothed and supported his body once more.

"Will he eat, do you think?" asked another of the voices in the night.

There was no answer to this most vital question. Not until the next day would the trainers know if the catch had been for nothing.

The simple act of eating is the first and most important step in a dolphin's training.

What the humans knew (and Gordo could not) was that a dolphin who refuses to eat is in a position of power. He must either be force-fed forever or returned to the sea.

6
Horror — and Hope

*I*n the morning, in the back section of the park, which visitors seldom see, Gordo waited quietly in the small training tank. Yesterday his whole world had changed. And today . . . ?

Footsteps crunched in gravel. Plastic boots approached. Red buckets were lifted onto the concrete poolside.

Plop! Something shining landed in the water beside the dolphin's face. Gordo was hungry, but he ignored the shimmering fish falling slowly now beside him. It didn't move as if it were alive, and Gordo had never eaten dead fish. He liked only the freshest of fish, snatched alive from their frantic dash to escape. What did he want with —

Smack! This time the butterfish thrown by the trainer

slapped against his jaw. In a sudden flash of irritation Gordo snapped. The fish he bit in anger broke, and juices flooded the dolphin's mouth.

Gordo swallowed. And with that bite, his chance for freedom fled. Had he not eaten, the humans would have had no practical choice but to set him loose. But once he accepted that first fish, the trainers knew they could keep him.

Gordo loved his food. As if he had done it this way for years, the giant dolphin snagged and gulped down fish after fish after fish. At first he swallowed them individually, a mere one at a time. Then he appeared to realize that the act of swallowing was slowing his consumption. After that he took as many as he could cram into his mouth, and swallowed only when the fish quit dropping from the sky — or wherever Gordo thought the fish were falling from.

"Eating pretty well, huh?" I asked his personal trainer, Dave Sweeney.

"Yeah, like a pig. They're calling him Gordo — 'fat one' in Spanish — and it's a good name for him. That's how he'll be if he keeps eating like that."

The first day, the man with the bucket came four times. Every time he threw a fish to Gordo, he blew a whistle.

At first Gordo jerked his head away from the fish when the whistle blew. But after a while he didn't mind the noise. In fact, he came to like it, as a cowboy likes the dinnerbell whose clanging calls him to his meals.

At the end of each visit, called a session, the trainer swooped his spread hands back and forth like an umpire signaling "safe," which meant the training was over.

In six months, if all went well, Gordo would be a part of the show.

Not long after Gordo arrived, Ernestine became ill.

At first we thought it was sadness, grief over her loss of Lucky, that made Ernestine stop eating and lose interest in leaping for the shows. Unlike wolves and sometimes people, dolphins do not mate for life, but they do form very strong emotional attachments to one another.

But then the trainers noticed something small, so small that it seemed of little importance. Some odd, squarish, rough patches had appeared on Ernestine's sides — little marks like wind-chapping. They looked almost like small pieces of transparent tape, faintly discolored, stuck to her sides.

"I hope that's not what I think it is," said the vet. He ordered Ernestine pulled out as quickly as the divers could be called together.

"Erysipelas?" whispered the trainer, and the veterinarian just shook his head.

Erysipelas. An acutely infectious disease of the skin and mucous membrane glands, said to have wiped out whole herds of dolphins in the wild.

Ernestine let herself be caught without trouble, which was not like her.

We carried her over to the flume tank, a shallow rectangular pool between the dolphin grotto and the larger reef aquarium tank.

A set of stadium bleachers had been built over the flume,

and one end had been blocked off so it was now an extension of the reef: a quiet place, shaded by the floor of the dolphin-show bleachers overhead.

Not much happened in the flume tank, normally. Once in a while a salt truck would back up to it and deposit a half-ton pile of salt crystals, which would first look like diamonds, then snow, then melting slush as it slowly dissolved, keeping the reef tank salted for the fish.

Now Ernestine would be there. We dared not allow her within touching distance of the other dolphins, lest they, too, catch her deadly sickness. The people in the bleachers above had no way of knowing that only a few feet below them a dolphin was fighting for her life — fighting against a cold, implacable, unfeeling enemy.

We blocked the reef end of the flume to prevent her from getting in with the turtles and the fish. I would have liked to let her swim among them, but it would have been extremely difficult to catch her in there — something we would have to do several times a day now, so the vet could give her injections and take blood samples.

Something like a horror movie began to take place.

The rectangular patches on her side were called plaques, and they began to spread, and to change. Darkening. Bulging. Until one day when I was holding Ernestine, and she struggled suddenly, and I tightened my grip just a little, the soft ends of my fingers slipped through the plaques and into her flesh.

Frightened, I straightened my fingers out and away from her. The gray skin came with them. I looked into the wounds and saw that, beneath the plaques, the flesh was liquefying, rotting into drooling putrescence.

It was as if acid were eating her away.

I could hardly think of the dolphins now without pain.

In the deep tank, Arnie beat us up every time we entered. Like a bully with a nightstick he pounded us, day after day.

And every day, three times a day, I had to hold Ernestine so the vet could do his work. In my mind I pleaded with her not to struggle, because when she did, pieces of her broke away, coming off on my hands, however gently I held her.

I almost wanted her to die. I didn't know if she felt pain or not, but the slightest movement tore her. Sometimes my hands would be clogged with fragments of her flesh. *Holes* appeared on her sides, at the back of her dorsal fin, in her gracefully sculptured crescent-shaped tailflukes. It was as though small sharks were eating her a little bit each day.

I hated the disease. I wished the erysipelas was something I could take into my hands and choke, to make it stop hurting Ernestine.

Sometimes when we went in to see her, the other dolphins would be lined up on the other side of the concrete wall, and she and they would be facing each other. Perhaps they were hearing sonar noises through the concrete, I don't know. But it felt like a hospital scene, when relatives visit, and wait, because there's nothing they can do but just be there.

I wondered how life could just keep going on as if this suffering were not happening. Couldn't the traffic jams and hassles of life slow down for a while, until we knew whether Ernestine would live or die?

But the cruelty and the strength of life is that it does go on, regardless.

Even Gordo's training continued. It had to be hurried, in fact, because there was an urgent need for another dolphin at topdeck, with Lucky gone and Ernestine's future . . . uncertain.

Gordo was not what you could call a natural show animal. He was willing enough, said Dave Sweeney, his trainer, but, well, there were problems.

The first part of the training had gone okay because Gordo simply loved to eat. Once he understood that the whistle meant fish, the eternally ready-to-eat guylli would do a great deal to bring on that whistle sound.

With the "bridge" between whistle and food established, the next step was "approximation."

To understand how this works, think of that old guessing game Hot or Cold, in which an object is hidden in a room, and the players are told they are "hot" when they move close to the object and "cold" when they go away from it. That is how approximation works. Any step in the right direction is rewarded with a whistle and a fish. Going in the wrong direction means no reward.

To get Gordo to "target" — to put his beak on a small white ball on the end of a stick — Sweeney first rewarded the dolphin for simply swimming toward him. Then, like a camera sharpening its focus, better and better behavior would be required before a reward was given. The trainer would say, "Target . . . target . . . ," holding the foam ball on the end of the stick in the water as the dolphin came toward it. Then he would reward him only for holding still next to the target, and finally only when Gordo touched it.

When Gordo learned to target on command, everything else was built on that.

Want to teach a dolphin to flip? Begin with the target, and call your dolphin over, saying, "Target . . . target. . . ." When the dolphin arrives and places its beak against the target, make it keep its beak there while you move the target in a slow circle underwater. The dolphin follows the circle — and that begins the movement of a flip. By rewarding the dolphin with the whistle and a fish when it performs the first stage of the flip, and by always doing the same voice command and hand signal, you let the dolphin know when the flip is wanted.

A very important show signal is the hand motion for the leap, which looks like the trainer is throwing a short bullet football pass. This movement began with the throwing of a fish, which naturally Gordo enjoyed. When the trainer moved his hand that certain way, food flew. Then one day the trainer made the short throwing motion, and Gordo jumped to get the fish — but there was no fish!

Instead, the whistle blew, and when Gordo returned to the stage, he was "heavily reinforced," which meant he got about eight fat herring as quick as he would take them in. The dolphin learned that a hand signal from a trainer, if he acted upon it correctly, could make the food fall out of the sky, and he liked that part a very great deal.

The rest of the training process was mainly repetition and variation, the way a dancer endlessly practices her or his craft, exercising and learning new steps. When Gordo firmly understood one behavior, variations on it would be added. When he could swim across a rope on the bottom of the tank without getting nervous, the rope would be raised, higher and higher, until he learned to leap across it in a show. These variations added to the number of things the dolphin could do in a show and also helped to keep him interested.

But, well, as his trainer put it, there were problems with Gordo.

The ideal show dolphin is smallish, curious, energetic, and eager to please.

Gordo, however, was big and getting bigger. He was also easygoing and a trifle on the clumsy side (if truth be told), and his idea of a great time was to get his belly scratched. The idea that he should trade dedicated labor for food went against the inclinations of his personality.

However, there was a need for a dolphin up at topdeck, and Gordo was elected.

On a windy afternoon several months later, we set a sagging stretcher on the edge of the dolphin show pool.

"Wait till he breathes," the vet commanded, and everybody sat around scratching as the dolphin held his breath, which dolphins tend to do in situations of stress.

The reason behind the practice of waiting till the dolphin breathes is that it must wake for every breath of its life, and an unconscious dolphin can die if it's dropped into the water. But to make a wide-awake animal wait in the discomfort of gravity, balanced on a narrow concrete wall, always struck me as an unnecessary hassle for everyone concerned, especially the dolphin.

TOOO-HUHHHP! No question whose giant breath that was.

"Okay, let him go!"

We flipped the canvas back, freeing the huge dolphin inside.

Gordo saw the water rippling blue below him, and nobody had to tell him what to do next. Even before we tilted the far side of the stretcher to give him an assist, the giant dolphin had heaved himself sideways and was crashing into instantly created foam. Everybody cheered to see the dolphin enter his new home.

But in the instant Gordo fell, a streak of darkness answered, so fast that there was an audible hiss as the dorsal fin knifed through the surface.

How nice, I thought: one of the dolphins is coming to welcome Gordo. I could hardly have been more wrong.

It was Arnie.

Like a rabid wolverine he charged, and Gordo's larger size meant nothing. Tremendous tailslaps were heard, audible even from under water. Gordo fought back as best he could, but the sheer ferocity of Arnie overwhelmed him, and presently the larger dolphin was on the run, with Arnie right behind him.

"They'll just have to work it out," said one of the trainers.

They never did work it out, not really. Sometimes they appeared to have reached an agreement, even to the point where Gordo appeared to be carrying out Arnie's commands. Jim Mullen told me that Gordo would sometimes act as Arnie's gangsterlike bodyguard! "Go beat up Delbert," Arnie seemed to say, moving his beak, indicating the shark-scarred dolphin — and Gordo would instantly go fight with him. But sooner or later Arnie and Gordo would forget

any temporary truce, and the two would start fighting again.

To everyone's surprise, however, Gordo's training suddenly improved.

In spite of Arnie's harassment, or perhaps because of it, Gordo began to do behaviors that till then had seemed impossible for him. Sometimes a dominant dolphin will insist that a new dolphin learn the behaviors *right away*, and this may well have been the case with Arnie and Gordo.

Dave Sweeney put a hoop in the water and got Gordo to swim through it by placing the target on the far side. Then the trainer raised the hoop. When the hoop was about

eight feet above the water and the dolphin was still jumping through it, the trainer turned a switch and an unseen jet of gas rushed through the hollow hoop. A lighter ignited the gas, and soon Gordo was leaping through a hoop of flames.

The fire part was actually easy. Being a water creature, Gordo had no idea what fire was. Since he was wet and passed through the small flames quickly, he didn't even feel the heat, except perhaps like sunshine brushing his wet hide.

The big dolphin learned to leap almost twenty feet above the surface of the pool to get a fat blue mackerel on the end of a pole. But as I said, he was a trifle clumsy. As often as not he would bite the pole and pull it down along with the fish.

Once he brought something else in, too. Trainer Dave Sweeney was crouching on the stage one day during a show, and perhaps he was a little distracted by something or someone in the audience. Well, Gordo apparently decided he wanted Dave's attention. He got it, too. The giant dolphin clambered up and propped his fins on the trainer's shoulders. The audience loved it as trainer joined dolphin for an unscheduled swim.

As the weeks went by and Gordo gained confidence, he began to assert himself against Arnie, to fight back against the smaller but more aggressive animal. They would slash and rake each other's skin with their needle-sharp teeth and fight swirling, chasing duels back and forth across the tank. Arnie would always win, as Lucky always had over him, but the fights continued.

Eventually the brawling became so serious that the water had to be lowered, and both dolphins had their teeth ground down. This sounds much worse than it is. Dolphin teeth are not like human teeth, which are filled with highly sensitive nerves and pulp. Dolphin teeth are solid and have no more nerve endings than human hair, which can be cut without pain to its owner. The little buzzing grinder looked and sounded awful, but it did the animals no harm and prevented them from tearing one another up. They could and would still fight with thumping blows of head and tail, but at least their delicate skin would not be ripped and torn.

Teeth dulled or not, however, Arnie continued to make the divers' lives miserable.

Imagine for a moment that you have to scrub a floor —

and you absolutely have to scrub it or lose your job — but there is a 350-pound bully with a policeman's nightstick in the room all the time. He can hit you whenever he wants to, and he apparently wants to most of the time. How would you feel about this individual, even if everyone else thought he was wonderful?

Arnie, the assassin: that was how I thought of him.

As if my problems with Arnie weren't enough, every day when I went to work I expected to hear that Ernestine had died.

One day we were standing in the shadows of the flume tank. It felt like a dark forest. The beams of the bleachers above us were like crossed boughs, and the light seemed filtered as if through leaves.

In the waist-deep water we held her: Ernestine.

She began to kick and I felt a spark of hope. She hadn't fought for a long time. But the flash of hope quickly dimmed when I saw what the struggle was doing to her, where my fingers touched her flesh.

"No, babe, hold still, you're hurting yourself," I said, blinking rapidly, turning away from the other divers so they would not see my face.

But Ernestine kept on wriggling, struggling, fighting, and the rotten skin kept coming away . . . and then I saw it.

Clean, fresh, marbled, black-and-gray hide, smooth and soft and flexible, growing taut and strong beneath the ugliness.

New skin!

Afraid to let myself hope, lest my hopes be broken again, I brushed off another of the scabby rotten places, and the ugliness seemed drier somehow, like old newspaper rolling in shreds. And underneath it? Yes! More new skin!

The disease had reached the limits of its power. The dolphin's strength was asserting itself.

When I walked out of the shadowed flume after that, I knew my Ernestine was going to be all right, and I didn't care the least little bit what my eyes were doing.

7

How Smart Are Dolphins?

*E*rnestine was back!

She had scars on her sides, but nothing you would notice unless you knew where to look. Her dorsal fin had lost a half-moon of flesh, and her tailflukes looked like a shark had caught up with one side, but the wounds were all healed and cleanly seam-edged. More important, the spirit beneath seemed untouched. Ernestine's beauty was inside as well as out; the part of her that really mattered was undiminished by her sufferings.

Along with Ernestine's recovery came more good news. Marine World's management had decided to create a new dolphin exhibit, to be called the Porpoise Petting Pool, for dolphin-human interaction. There would be no shows in the petting pool at all. It would be a small, figure-eight-shaped pool, deep at both ends with a dividing ridge in the middle. One side would be open to the public; the other would be blocked off by bushes and lava rock. A thatched roof high above would keep the sun off.

People could get close to the dolphins, even touch one, if both species wanted. If a dolphin wished no more human company for a while, he or she could just stay away from the people's edge of the pool.

There would be two new animals, Terry and Spray (former show dolphins from another park), residing in the petting pool, but more important to me, *Arnie would be going there!* The dolphin grotto would be a peaceful place again with him out of the way. And the petting pool would be small and easy to clean, I figured, so my time with Arnie would be cut way back.

In fact, for six months or a year, I probably wouldn't have to go in and clean Arnie's new pool at all. Brand-new paint goes on real slick and smooth, so it would be a while before it roughened up enough for the algae to catch on.

It was a chore catching Arnie, of course, and he broke my mask lens for me, smacking that hard beak of his against the heavy plastic so hard a crack shot like lightning across it, and I did the rest of the grab with water rushing in and out of my nose.

But it didn't matter. Catching that dolphin was one of the most satisfying moments of my life. I had taken so much heat from him. Now to feel my arms lock around his chest, and stare into his red-brown eye, and feel the frustrated rage boiling at me the same way I felt when he had swum around and beaten me up day after day after day, and me helpless to do anything about it . . . well, it was a pleasure.

Now, I thought, with Arnie out of the way for a while, I'll get a chance to find out what dolphins are really like. I might even be able to figure out a better answer to the second-most-popular question Marine World divers get.

When people found out I worked for Marine World, the first question they usually asked was, How dangerous are sharks? This was not impossible to answer, because I had only to point to the ocean. On any hot summer day, millions of swimmers went into the sea, and of course the sharks didn't go away. That was their home, and they went right on with their normal lives, sometimes cruising calmly right underneath the feet of the people. If sharks were like the monsters in the movies, the oceans would be red with human blood. Instead, shark attack is extraordinarily rare. Around the whole world, perhaps a dozen people die by shark each year, far fewer than are killed by lightning bolts — not to mention such genuinely horrific killers as automobiles on the freeway!

The second question was almost always, How smart are dolphins?

I knew that their brains were shaped very much like our own, and of a similar size. I also knew that it wasn't just that they needed big brains for their sonar system; otherwise bats would have bigger skulls, for these flying creatures also use echolocation: finding out where they are in darkness by making noise, listening to the echoes, and locating themselves by the sound.

But how smart are dolphins? As the months went by and became years, many strange things happened, but I felt no nearer to the answer.

Take Mr. Spock, for instance.

Sometimes this dolphin's mental capacity seemed positively uncanny — almost like that of his namesake, the pointy-eared, intellectual Vulcan from TV's *Star Trek*. At other times, though, he behaved like a total airhead.

Sometimes Spock would swim down to the bottom of the tank when I was scrubbing. The powerfully built, sleek animal would offer me his dorsal fin, and we would first go for a little ride. Spock unquestionably gave the best dolphin rides in town. His body mass was great enough to break a big "hole" in the water, so as to tow a human more easily, and we would go so fast!

I felt the way a high-diver would feel if, when he cleaves through the water perfectly after a thirty-foot fall, he could somehow keep that momentum going. My speed shot from its normal, miserable little two miles an hour (if that much) to maybe twenty. Imagine having your swimming speed boosted by a multiple of ten!

And then something quiet but strange and wonderful would happen. Spock would take me up to the surface in the middle of the tank and just stop.

At first I didn't understand. I thought I had somehow irritated or offended him, and I let go. But the dolphin came and got me again and took me back up, to what I gradually realized was his favorite part of the tank. This was a sort of club spot, a high-status dolphin place. There were no currents here to deal with, and no filtration noise. The sun shone directly on us; it was warm and peaceful, and we were free to do . . . almost nothing.

We would just lie there, floating. I would drop my belt and let it clunk all the way down to the bottom. My arm was touching but not restricting him, loose on his smooth-muscled back. I could lie either on my back or on my belly, snoozing almost, breathing the air through my mouthpiece.

The peace I felt was warm and complete. It seemed right, the way things should be. We were not human and animal, not owner and pet. No. This was different.

As J. Allen Boone put it in his classic book, *Kinship with All Life,* we were no longer separated by the artificial labels of species but were simply "two life forms, experiencing the universe," together.

When it came time to play, Spock was both ready and inventive. Once when I took the heavy metal grate from the disconnected drain in the center of the deep pool, Spock used his rostrum to push the heavy thing across the floor until it fell, *clunk,* into place. He enjoyed this small game immensely and would often drag me over to make me take the grate out just so he could push it in again. For variety I would stand the heavy object up so he could knock it over and then manipulate it into place.

Sometimes the grate would catch on something, and he wouldn't quite be able to figure out the required combination of shoves and nudges to make it fit the square slot. When that happened he would poke me, and I would add a nudge or two myself, as my contribution to solving the problem.

I enjoyed playing "shove" with either Spock or Ernestine.

I would hold my hand up, and Spock would plant his beak squarely in the center of my palm and stiffen his body like a spear; then I would shove. Even backwards, the dolphin streamlining is so perfect that the animal can glide fifteen or twenty feet on the strength of one (exhausting) shove. Then Spock would give a trifling little kick and be back for more. I preferred playing this with Ernestine because of her lighter bodyweight and lesser mass. But at least Spock wouldn't beat me up when I got too tired to continue, as Arnie had sometimes done.

It was Spock who taught me "top jaw—bottom jaw" by raising and lowering his beak swiftly over my fingers and then mouthing them gently. Once I understood what was wanted, the game was fun for both of us: a re-creation of the fish-catching motion for him, an eye-hand coordination test for me. The idea was for me to move my hand from above his top jaw to below his bottom jaw — without being caught between the white teeth. Now his control could be seen. I was never crunched, never badly torn up. The worst that happened was that sometimes the outer edge of Spock's jaw would chomp rather painfully on my finger ends, or every once in a while I might go a little too quickly for accuracy and shove one of his gleaming white teeth beneath a fingernail, which smarted.

It was also Spock who invented the dolphin bank account.

Trainer Jim Mullen was worried that a dolphin might die from swallowing a paper cup or some other trash a thoughtless human might knock into the pool, so the trainer worked out a deal with Spock: any piece of trash the dolphin brought to Jim would be traded for a fish.

One day Mr. Spock showed up at stage-side with an inch-long scrap of brown paper lying on his large pink tongue. He reared up out of the water, demanding payment.

Mullen honored the agreement, going to a nearby refrigerator to fetch a fish for Spock.

Five minutes later, Spock was back with another teensy ragged piece of brown paper.

Okay, another fish, and then another — but where were all these little bitty scraps of brown paper coming from?

Jim sent a diver down to check things out, and sure enough, there in the corner of the tank was a large brown paper bag and some string. Spock was tearing off one tiny piece of paper at a time and trading it for fish.

Isn't that pretty close to the concept of money?

Yet it was also this same "smart" dolphin who swallowed an eight-inch stainless-steel bolt left standing on the floor by a diver who'd been doing repair work on a filtration pipe.

Why would a dolphin want to swallow a stainless-steel bolt? It was plainly of limited food value! But a more serious and immediate question was, How are we going to remove the sharp-pointed object?

We caught Mr. Spock, took him to the vet clinic, and laid him on the operating table.

While I knelt in the sink (that being the only place where I could get a good angle to stabilize his tail), the vet tech assistant (ironically, his name was Ron Swallow) stuck a Vaseline-coated arm right down the dolphin's throat, into its first stomach. He felt the sharp tip of the bolt, but the dolphin gulped it down deep, into the second stomach, just out of reach.

"My arm's not long enough," Ron Swallow said.

We couldn't get the bolt. But we had to, or else the sharp point might tear the lining of the dolphin's stomach. We dared not use pliers or other mechanical extenders, for these too might tear the delicate tissue.

What about an operation? In those days it was impossible. Dolphins must be conscious to breathe. Even at night, they have to wake a little for each separate breath. Nowadays special pumps can artificially inflate dolphin lungs during an operation, but we didn't have those yet.

But what about a person with a very long arm? Like a basketball player? Mary Jo O'Herron Ball, the park's publicity person, knew a player with the Golden State Warriors.

In an hour, a seven-foot, two-inch black giant stooped through the doorway of the vet clinic. He was willing to put his career on the line to try and save a dolphin's life. If Spock panicked and bit down harder than the towel-holding people were ready for, it would only take one sharp tooth cutting into the athlete's biceps, maybe even severing a ligament, to limit the player's subtle control of the limb and thereby end his career in professional sports.

Nonetheless, into the mouth and down the animal's throat went the athlete's fingers, and his wrist, and that endless arm. Deeper, deeper. We feared the bolt had gone into the third stomach, out of reach, which would almost certainly mean death. The athlete's shoulder touched the inside of the dolphin's jaws; nothing further could be done.

And then the man looked up, and smiled.

"I think I got it," he said, and when he withdrew his Vaseline-slick arm, the gleaming deadly object was right there, safe and harmless in his hand. The room overflowed with happy laughter and cheers.

And this was how Clifford Ray became Marine World/ Africa USA's favorite basketball player, then and for always.

How intelligent are dolphins? I can't say for sure, but even the old assassin himself seemed pretty smart . . . or should I say crafty?

Though I didn't spend much time with Arnie after we moved him from the show pool, I did have to go into the petting pool every now and then to clean uneaten fish off the drain. Before climbing in I would naturally watch him for a while, trying to figure out his mood. But, like Lucy in the comic strip "Peanuts," holding the football for Charlie Brown and promising that this time, *this time* she won't yank it away, Arnie would always fake me out.

He never showed the slightest hint of irritability when I leaned over the edge of the pool. On the contrary, he would appear glad to see me, gliding over so nicely, offering his belly for a rub. I would sit on the edge of the pool with my feet in the water, letting him know that I was going to come into the pool, while scratching his stomach and giving him all the attention a dolphin could ask for.

In a couple of minutes, Arnie would seem to grow bored and would kick casually off to the other side of the tank. Watching him very closely, I would climb into the water, still keeping one hand on the wall. When he showed no signs of interest, I'd let go of the side, watch for a few seconds, and swim a little distance from the wall. Maybe this time he was going to be nice. When I got out to the middle, I would hold my breath, take one last look at Arnie, and dive down to the drain.

BAM! He'd hit me like a thrown bowling ball. Faked out again. I would have to curl up on my back, trying to keep track of the bumping, ramming, raking, tail-slapping dolphin while I clutched for the fish on the drain. (It wasn't that he cared about the fish, either, because he would do the same thing if I went in to pull out blown-in pine needles or leaves.)

Time and again he would trick me, revealing none of the usual signals of anger or aggression. He wouldn't arch his back, or snap his jaws, or bark, or slash his head from side to side or up and down, or in any way reveal what he seemed to be planning. No, he was Mr. Goodnatured Dolphin . . . until I got just far enough away from the safety of the walls.

With only body language and behavior to judge by, it was impossible to know for sure what was going on inside a dolphin's mind.

Was it my imagination that a female dolphin named Shiloh developed a sort of "crush" on me? I never knew for sure if I understood the situation right, but the dolphin appreared to be jealous. She would beat up female divers when they went into the tank with me, but she left them alone if I was out. One woman diver, Lindy Cook, had to be denied that tank altogether; we traded her responsibility for the eel tank instead. I don't remember anyone envying her the trade; I was certainly never overjoyed about sharing space with forty slithery moray eels!

Another woman diver, named Roberta Quist, arrived several years later and was the best "dolphin person" I ever knew. In a crowd of people standing by the petting pool, dolphins would single her out to visit. She apparently had the ability to make a dolphin feel as if it were the center of the universe. But Shiloh gave Roberta trouble too, sneaking over at every opportunity to give her a thump, although she'd often stop if I looked up from my scrubbing in time. I finally had to "introduce" the two females of different species. Taking Bert by the arm and Shiloh by the pec fin and holding them close together, I tried to let Shiloh know the human was okay. I felt a little silly doing it, but Shiloh did grow less aggressive toward her.

So much is guesswork with dolphins! I have heard people say that dolphin sonar is so powerful and precise that they can "look" into the body of a diver or another dolphin and recognize hormone levels or gastric upsets. I have no idea if this is true or not.

Some people think dolphins communicate by thought waves: telepathy.

A respected trainer named Frank Robson relates in his book, *Talking Dolphins, Singing Whales,* how he ran an entire dolphin show by telepathy, telling the dolphins what to do by mental commands alone. I asked trainer Jim Mullen about this, and he believed that Robson, an honorable man, may have unconsciously given the dolphins tiny body-language signals. The dolphins may have picked up cues too small and subtle for the trainer to realize he was giving. I didn't know.

One researcher claimed to be in mental contact with some

of our dolphins, one named Dondi in particular. One day diver John Racanelli asked the researcher if he had had any news from Dondi lately, and the researcher said, oh yes, he had, and told how Dondi said this and that and the other thing, and Racanelli said that was very interesting, especially since the dolphin in question had recently died.

I didn't poke much fun at anybody's dolphin beliefs, though. I couldn't logically explain some of my own opinions.

And once I did feel that the dolphins were reading my mind.

I had had a long-standing wrestling challenge with a diver and ocean-animal-sculptor friend named Alan Therkelsen. We would stand on the dolphin stage in our wetsuits and laboriously struggle back and forth. We were an even match: sometimes one would win, sometimes the other.

But on this particular day, Alan was the victor and I was flung off my feet and into the water.

I had an ear infection that was really troubling me, and my left eardrum was inflamed and throbbing. I hit the water exactly wrong, and it was excruciating when the water cracked against the sensitive ear.

In my mind, I screamed.

Instantly the four dolphins came up to me, and I thought they wanted to play, to take me under for a dive as they so often did. I said *in my mind,* "No, no, I'm hurting. I can't go under, leave me alone!"

They didn't leave me alone. Neither did they play with me. Instead, Ernestine, Gordo, Spock, and Delbert swam directly underneath me, so that I was perched in a semi-sitting posture, and they rushed me to the side of the tank.

There they gave me one great shove, so that I was out of the tank almost before my hands touched the side.

"Did you see what happened?" I asked Alan, a bit unsure myself.

"They picked you up," he said. "Do they do this often?"

"No, this is the first time," I said. It was the last time, too.

I will always believe that the dolphins knew I was in trouble and tried to help me. How did they know? I can only repeat: I don't know.

I remember how excited I was when John and Antonietta Lilly came to the park and set up Project Janus, named after the Greek god with two faces, symbolizing the meeting of human and dolphin minds. John Lilly was the first person to systematically try to communicate with the dolphins, and we wished him all the best.

Sometimes it seemed he was so close. His assistant, computer expert John Kert, set up a van with a massive computer terminal. Using microphones leading into the computer and from there to hydrophones in the water, the Lillys hoped humans and dolphins would be able to talk to each other. Every day the people tried, while at the same time they also had to work constantly to raise the money needed to keep the project going.

Once I heard that a dolphin had spoken so clearly in an imitation of John Kert's voice that even with the computer the words were clear and that Kert's Hungarian accent could be detected.

Naturally I wanted to hear that and asked to listen to the tape. It didn't sound like human talk to me. I couldn't distinguish anything in it, although the people standing beside me apparently could. Maybe it's like listening to people from other places, whom at first you can't understand even though they're speaking your own language. On slowed-down tape recordings I had heard dolphins say numbers in squeaky, parrotlike voices, but this noise sounded like garbled bubbles to me, and I could make nothing of it.

From what I could see, the great breakthrough did not happen.

But even if this experiment wasn't a complete success, like a pioneer in the wilderness, Lilly took some giant steps into the unknown. By daring to think hugely he freed others: to dream and to develop new ways of exploring an intelligence alien to our own.

How smart are dolphins? It's hard to say, because their lives are so different from ours. Even among humans it's impossible to say who's the most intelligent. Is a poet smarter than a lawyer? Who knows more, the carpenter or the real estate salesperson? Each mind follows a different path and is intelligent according to its different needs.

Human achievement is based on our use of our fingers and thumb and the tools that are extensions of those digits. With our fingers and thumb we write, steer speedboats, shovel custard cake into our mouths, and fine-tune the reception of color TV sets. Almost everything we do starts and finishes with hand and tool use.

But dolphin fingers are hidden in their pectoral fins, and they almost never use tools. One time a dolphin at Marineland of Florida picked up a scorpionfish in its mouth and pushed it under a reef to force out a moray eel that the dolphin wanted to chase. But the few, rare exceptions like this one only show how difficult and awkward tool use is for them.

Humankind's technology brings change; that is natural for us. We are the guardians and gardeners of Earth. It is our natural job to look after the place and hopefully to leave it better than it was when we arrived.

But the dolphin needs no tools. In its environment it can be successful without technology, almost without bringing change at all. The dolphin swims and eats and reproduces and dies, making no mark on its blue world.

I believe dolphins appreciate beauty and take joy in many things, including the balletic exercise of their own swimming motions. Sometimes they change the way they swim for no apparent reason but amusement: they swim upside down or even do an "Australian crawl," hauling themselves through the water with laughably awkward "arm strokes" of their pectoral fins, completely opposite their normal tail-surging grace.

Ernestine was truly a dolphin artist. She could arch her upper body and make three bubble rings in quick succession, each slightly larger than the one before, so that they fit around each other and arrived at the surface like a target with concentric rings. She could also spin a giant bubble ring, making the shimmering, mercurial object wobble and vibrate but not break. It held its luminous unity, and as the pretty thing rose, Ernestine spun it out and whittled off the edges, making it smaller and smaller.

How smart are dolphins?

How smart is the bee as it walks across the blinding

beauty of a flower and afterwards wings its way home to dance before the others in the hive in a way that tells them how to get to the flower, to the source of the pollen the bees must have to continue life?

What does the snake know when it glides in supple grace across the forest floor, in intimacy with the roots of trees and leaves and earth, and by flicking its tongue follows the scent trails (just molecules in air!) of mice and rats, whose population the reptile keeps under control?

What does the utterly brainless mosquito understand when it descends in hordes to suck the blood of Alaskan caribou, and by its millions of irritating stings keeps those reindeer on the move . . . so that as the snow melts and the new plants rise, the deer do not stay in any one place long enough to munch the vegetation's roots down to the ground and strip the earth?

Some will say this is not intelligence at all, but mere instinct — as if calling what animals do "instinct" and what people do "intelligence" makes us somehow better than they are.

But there are different — and conflicting — definitions of intelligence, even in the dictionary. Is intelligence the size of the mind, or the amount of information it contains? Is it the container or the contents that's important? Is the brain different from the mind?

I don't know. Does anyone? Can we know for sure what goes on in the consciousness of any life form? Plants have none of what we call nerve endings, yet they reach toward water and shrink from flame. Do they feel? Can we say with certainty that a redwood tree, which stands and grows for a thousand years, has no consciousness at all?

We need to think of other life forms as of value like our own, or else we will never stop wrecking the planet. If we truly considered every life form to be important, for instance, we would hesitate before dumping poison in the sea, where it kills microorganisms that add oxygen to air and form the base of our food chain.

How smart are dolphins? I cannot tell you. I only know that whether they are smart like people, or just smart like dolphins, I love them just the way they are.

8

To Ernestine

*E*rnestine lay lightly across the tops of my feet. Her back was getting dry and I splashed a little water onto it as we rested together in the shallow portable pool. Dark clouds overhung the sky, and I could not see the stars.

Almost midnight. Time to do a respiration count, I thought, and reached from my half-wet chair, across the dolphin with the scars, there where she rested between my shins and the plastic liner of the portable pool.

From where she was, all Ernestine could see was one of my wetsuited legs and the wall.

Taking the watch from the railing, I waited for her to breathe.

This was the third week she had been ill. As her kind

would have done for her in the wild, we had been watching her around the clock. As she grew weaker, we kept her upright in the water so that her blowhole wouldn't slip under and cause her to drown.

Puhhhhaaaiiip. The exhale, inhale, and closing of the blowhole sounded like three disjointed actions instead of the single crisp operation it was supposed to be. And the breath was no longer the clean summer air of a healthy dolphin. It smelled bad. This wasn't a skin disease like erysipelas, but something deep inside.

"You've been this sick before and got better, babe!" I said, more for myself than for her.

She was so beautiful, even now, eyes closed, so strangely still. The scars remained: the holes through the clean perfection of her flukes and one pectoral; the half-moon chunk taken from her dorsal; the blurred recessions on her side, where the wounds had healed. But that was only wrapping. I loved the life within her, the part that could never be touched by scars.

I dipped my hand in the water and wet her, lest the warm skin dry and crack. During the day, we draped wet towels over her and used a homemade awning to keep the sun away.

"We've been through some great times together, haven't we?" I felt the need to talk, as if at the bedside of somebody I loved who now was — I talked, to stop the thoughts, the realization of what was inevitably to come.

"Hey, remember that time you kept Lucky from beating me up?" I said. "Of course, you got me a good one yourself once in a while. 'Member when you broke my ear?"

I had been trying to catch her once in deep water, and

she had turned and warned me, warned me with every means she had — hunching her body, snapping her jaws, moving her head — and when I came ahead anyway, she did a sort of forward roll. Her tail came over and around and caught me at the side of the head with an impact like a car crash, lifting me half my body's length out of the water. As I sank back down, I heard a whistling noise as the water entered through my ruptured eardrum.

I was still half-deaf in that ear, but that couldn't be held against her. She had let me know what was going to happen if I kept pressing her. I should have backed off for a while, given her time to calm down, change her mind.

She was so strong! I remembered the first time I caught her in shallow water. Her tail felt like a swung construction beam as it knocked me off my feet, and for forty-five minutes we five husky divers couldn't hold that one small dolphin still for the vet.

Other memories flooded back, like the time I had tried to hide behind the petting-pool walls so that I could sneak up on Ernestine, who was temporarily staying there with the nonshow dolphins.

It had been early, and there was almost nobody else in the park. I heard the dolphins splashing in the petting pool from a long way off, and I thought: I wonder if I can sneak up on them. I had tennis shoes on, and you know you can walk very quietly indeed with rubber-soled shoes on if you work at it, and I did. Step by step, I set each foot down very softly, easing my weight onto it most gradually, never letting even the faintest sound (I thought) send vibrations of warning to the animals in the pool.

I crouched down so they couldn't see me either; I even

duck-walked with my legs far apart so that my pant legs wouldn't rustle against each other. Almost giggling at my own cleverness, I huddled at the low wall beside the pool. The dolphins stopped what they were doing. I didn't breathe.

Then about a gallon of water came over the edge of the pool to my right. Another wave sloshed over to my left, and for some reason I thought of the old artillery practice of lobbing one shell ahead of the target, then one behind it, and finally one right on the money. *Whooosh!* What felt like about half the pool leaped out and drenched me. Soaked to the skin, I jumped and hollered and swore, and laughed, and nobody can tell me dolphins have no sense of humor.

I remembered how Ernestine had loved Lucky, and how sometimes she or he would leap into the air and come back down, and the other would be waiting in the exact spot where that sleek shape would reenter and their bodies would brush. . . .

I remembered her wonderful endurance. She could be an incredibly difficult animal to catch when she set her mind to it. Sometimes she would just give right up — swim over to me and place herself in my arms. But other times!

Once she made me chase her for two hours, back and forth, from wall to wall, over the nets and back, again and again and again. I had gone to that point beyond fatigue where the body goes on automatic. Thus would I swim if a boat sank under me and I thought there might be an island somewhere near; I would swim until I made it or I died.

Died . . .

No.

I hid in memory, trying to turn back the clock, to bring

back the good times . . . like when I took my little girl, Desirée, into the tank with Ernestine.

Desirée Don, middle-named in pride after me, was two and a half years old. She wore a red and yellow Hawaiian-print swimsuit with small, crisp ruffles across the seat. Her mother wore a look of fixed anxiety — her baby going in with those animals! Despite the fact that our son, Roman, had recently taken up residence hugely inside her belly, my wife, Jeannie, waddled swiftly around the edge of the pool calling, "Watch out! Be careful!" and other such advice.

As I slipped into the water, shielding my baby with elbows and forearms and hunched shoulders, I realized I was really being stupid. I did so want her to meet and know dolphins . . . but Arnie was in the pool.

Still, I figured, if worse came to worst and Arnie attacked (which I didn't think he would because dolphins are, above all, curious about new things), then I would just shield Desirée with my body and hopefully absorb whatever damage I had to until I could lift her out.

Ernestine rushed over. For an instant I thought she meant trouble, but no, she was like a nice visiting lady bending over a baby carriage. Her gray snout edged inquisitively close, but not too close right away, as if she understood I was nervous. She appeared to grasp the situation perfectly. This was my little one, a young one of my kind; no threat was perceived or called for.

Introductions were in order, and as I said, "Hello, sweetheart," and reached out a tentative hand to stroke her (my gaze flicked to Arnie as he cruised in the background), Desirée said, "Hello, sweetheart," in her clear child's voice, and reached out a soft, tiny-boned hand. I heard my wife

suck in her breath at the side of the pool, there where her clutching hands kept trading places on the wall.

But Ernestine couldn't have been more courteous and considerate. She allowed her face to be touched, only flinching her eye tightly shut when Desirée accidentally poked her. For a moment, or perhaps a little longer, the two enjoyed each other's company.

Then Arnie rammed me in the right hip, where the muscle cups in and the hip joint operates. Bone met bone, and it was not a comic kick in the pants. I couldn't even swear or say ouch, because I was afraid Jeannie might think I had

lost control. "Things might get rough here, we better get out," I believe I said, and Desirée screamed and started struggling because she didn't want to get out.

I kicked for the wall, covering my daughter, aware that my spine was exposed to Arnie.

But Ernestine was there. As she had done that time against Lucky, again she stood between me and an angry dolphin. She shot beneath the surface and must have communicated something to Arnie — or hit him — because the arc of his charge veered off, and he surfaced on the far side of the tank from us. And now that dolphin did not try to hide his emotions. He snapped his jaws and puffed himself up and barked and made slashing motions with his teeth and in general acted very unpleasant indeed.

And to this day, my daughter remembers the kindness and courtesy of a sweet dolphin lady.

Ernestine gave me some of the most beautiful moments of my life, surpassed only by the births of my own children.

Children. As the thought bit in, the happiness faded, and I shivered in the night.

Ernestine should have had a calf, a young one of her own.

And she almost did. Almost.

It was a stillborn — a little calf, born dead, not breathing. It looked right: normal, though small, perfect in every way . . . except it was missing that sacred spark of life. The calf had fallen from her, down through the chill blue water, landing softly on the floor of the tank.

Ernestine did not understand, or would not accept it. She swam to the calf, picked it up across her rostrum, carried it to the air, and nudged it, trying to make it swim on its own. But the little flukes would not move. Ernestine tried everything she knew: poking, shoving, even nipping softly with her small teeth, trying to stimulate the calf to take that first breath.

But it didn't breathe, and in the end we knew we had to take the little body out.

A trainer tried to snatch the small form quickly when Ernestine passed the wall. She whipped him so hard with her tail that he was taken to the hospital and treated for a possible hairline fracture in his forearm.

She grew tired, and every so often she would leave the calf lying on the suction drain in the center of the floor while she went and breathed, making two and three trips around the tank, moving as if she were numb.

With scuba gear on, I hid behind nets in a corner underwater until Ernestine was at the farthest point from the center drain. Then I darted out, swimming as fast as I could.

It was only thirty or forty feet from the nets to the center of the pool. I reached the drain safely and put my hand on what lay there.

I had the small, still body in my arms and was rushing back when she turned. I knew when she turned because I heard her scream. And more. I felt the buzz of sonar brush the back of my bare neck. From the corner of my eye I saw her rushing toward me, and there was no way I could outswim her.

Three hundred pounds of fury driving in at ramming speed: in such manner had a dolphin killed a twenty-foot pilot whale at another oceanarium. She would snap my spine.

I could not think fast enough to drop what I carried, nor roll on my back. I just kept swimming, waiting to be rammed.

It did not happen. At the last instant, the dolphin turned away. I had taken the most precious part of life from her, but still she didn't harm me. After what had happened to her, no one could have blamed her for lashing out.

But she did not. As she had done so often, she gave me consideration, kindness I had no right to expect.

And how had I repaid her?

I looked at the featureless walls surrounding the two of

us. Here it was, the ugly something turning over in my mind, the thing I had tried so hard not to think about. Captivity.

I remembered what Jacques Cousteau said about oceanariums. The man I most respected in life, Cousteau was the co-inventor of the aqualung, author of many books, star of several TV shows, Academy Award–winning filmmaker, champion of the sea; the man who did more than anyone else to help people become aware of and enter the ocean. I loved Cousteau. In some ways I patterned my life after his. If I could be thought well of by any man on earth, it would be he.

And Jacques Cousteau's opinion of oceanariums? He called them "prison camps" that "deformed" the behavior of dolphins.

It was as if my family had disowned me, when I read that in one of his books.

I could stand against the disapproval of anyone, if I was just sure inside that I was right . . . but I was not so sure.

Ernestine was certainly not the only dolphin to have missed the experience of motherhood. A dolphin baby had never been born successfully at our park. In fact, in oceanariums almost everywhere, dolphin births were extremely rare.

Why? Dolphin females generally can't give birth until at least the age of seven; males generally can't father until they are fifteen or older. Though the average lifespan of a dolphin in captivity is now sixteen years, at that time it was between five and seven years, so it wasn't hard to see why so few dolphins reproduced.

Why don't dolphins in captivity live anywhere near as

long as the estimated thirty-five years they can live in the wild?

I thought I knew why. Better than anyone else, I knew at least one reason why.

It was the walls; those blank, featureless walls that I scrubbed every day.

Once I sat on the floor of the dolphin tank and just looked around, imagining what life would be like if I had to stay there, just *stay* in the tank for the rest of my time. I felt as if doors were being locked against me.

We took dolphins from the endless variety of the ocean and gave them an empty swimming pool: the sterility of boredom.

And four times a day the dolphins leaped for their food, and they smiled their permanent smiles, and I took my paycheck home on Fridays.

We were not mean. If a dolphin washed up on a nearby beach, Marine World would take care of it, though these animals almost always died. Generally dolphins don't beach themselves unless they are seriously ill, and then they may choose to die on the beach rather than be eaten by sharks. There was no profit in this for Marine World, but still we gave stranded dolphins the best chance we had in our power to give, feeding them and staying up with them all night; and it wasn't for publicity either, because after the first few dozen times it happens, dolphin-sitting becomes old stuff, and old stuff is not newsworthy. Greed for publicity was not why we tried to help.

Marine World was also a friend to dolphins in educating the public about them, helping people develop awareness of the sea, learning respect for the life of the wild.

We truly loved animals there. Even the boss, Mike De-metrios, was never happier than when he could escape for a while from the money problems that plague all zoos and aquariums and come help work with an animal. Twice he had put his own house up as collateral on a loan to keep Marine World alive.

No one worked there for the money, because the pay was terrible, starting off close to minimum wage and never rising very high.

I knew all the arguments for keeping animals on display: that they were ambassadors of their species, and that we learned from studying them. Before there were oceanariums, dolphins were routinely killed for oil or pet food or just because they were in the way, tangled in fishermen's nets. The Marine Mammal Protection Act, which prohibits or limits such slaughter, needs to be more strongly enforced, but it would never have even passed if millions of people hadn't gotten to see dolphins up close in oceanariums.

But none of that changed the fact that dolphins were kept in tanks with bare walls. I felt sure that this boredom stressed them, made some of them moody and bitter, and shortened their lives.

And I was a part of their captivity.

Ernestine kicked softly against my legs.

"Do you want to move around, go swimming?" I asked, straightening carefully so as not to put pressure on her sides.

Ernestine's swimming motions were strange — weak, but determined, and with a peculiar rhythm I did not remember having seen before.

I helped her swim to the deeper water at the center of the pool and let go.

But when I took my hands off the sick bottlenose dolphin, she opened her eyes, looked around her . . . and stopped. Her eyes closed. She rolled over on her side and would have sunk, but I was with her before her blowhole could slip under.

I raised her, awkwardly because we were in six feet of water and I did not have my fins on. Why had she seemed to want to swim, but then stopped when I gave her the chance? Maybe she wanted the feeling of motion but not the effort? That would be fine.

"Just let me get some fins, okay?" I said to her. I lugged her over to the chair and held her with one arm while I put my swimfins on.

The black cloud above us opened. We swam (or rather, I did, with Ernestine neither helping nor resisting) for an hour in the rain. It was not easy paddling in the middle, so I took my fins off after a while and walked around near the edges. There I could get footing, gripping with my toes on the ridged folds of the liner. It made no difference to Ernestine, as far as I could tell.

I stopped, finally, to take the respiration counts I had been forgetting and to let my own hard breathing catch up. I had turned the notebook over when the rain started. The fake wood clipboard had shielded the paper, but drops fell now as I wrote, and the words on the lines were blurred, as though by tears. I turned the notebook over and set it down.

Hemmed in gently between my legs and the liner, Ernestine again began to kick in the strange, new, peculiar rhythm: long strokes, rising and subsiding, as if tuned to the swells of the sea.

She looked like she was dreaming. Her eyes remained closed. There was no tension. The tail strokes rose and fell, rose and fell, revealing no haste, pushing on the down stroke, resting on the up-glide — the kind of swimming a dolphin might do if she was with her family pod once more and had a great distance to cover.

Perhaps she thought she was free.

I did not disturb her anymore. I only kicked the chart away behind me so that I could hold her with my arms.

There were no more sideward efforts to break loose; only the slowing waves of her flukes, their movement weakening, as if the tide were going out.

In a little while Ernestine convulsed, which is the last thing a dolphin does. I kept her from striking anything in the blindness of the little flurry. But it made no difference. She was past that now. Nothing could hurt her anymore.

The dolphin shuddered. There was a long, slow sigh as the air emptied out of her lungs. But this time there was no answering inhalation, just the too-long hiss of expiring air, and then the silence.

Ernestine was gone.

9

The Ultimate Danger

*I*t was five o'clock on a winter's afternoon. I stood at the edge of the dolphin petting pool.

In the distance I heard a lion: *Mwaaaoaaooh*. The roar echoed over the darkening, closed park. I knew it was only one of the Africa USA lions, hungry because once a week trainer Ron Whitfield fasted it for health reasons; the animal was not prowling loose. But still that groaning roar was an elemental noise, like the earth shaking.

Before me, indistinct in the awning shadows of his pool, was a hulking blur: 1,000 pounds of full-grown giant guylli dolphin.

"Hi, fat guy," I said, and my voice rang out too loudly,

like foolish bragging in the twilight. I spoke again, more softly.

"I've got to clean the fish off the drain, okay? It'll just take a minute."

I sat on the wooden edge and dangled my feet into the water.

I waited for any kind of a body-language signal from the dolphin in the pool. But he did not move. Was he setting me up like Arnie did? I wondered.

I tugged on my fins. The water was only four feet deep here, but I wanted mobility. A person in four feet of water can be pretty helpless if he loses his footing. I had to be able to move quickly — if Gordo was turning mean.

Holding my breath and closing my eyes, I slipped off the edge. The water closed over me and I fumbled my way toward the center drain. Keeping my eyes closed helped me to rely on other senses, rather than straining uselessly to see what couldn't be seen in the dark water.

My fingers slid along the floor, across the familiar cracks and crevices in the now-old paint. They stopped at the drain-plate cover. Up a quarter-inch, another inch or two across, and I felt the suction pulling through the stainless-steel drain-plate's holes, the water swirling down and through pipes below, into the turning blades of the impeller, and beyond into the filter leaves.

Then my sliding fingers touched something smooth: a fish, a Columbia River smelt, judging by the small-scaled texture of its skin, and another fish beside it, and another, a veritable heap of fish beside it. Gordo was hardly eating at all; he'd be losing weight if he —

Whooof! The air was knocked from my chest. Damn you,

Gordo, I said in my mind, rolling and coming up. My eyes blinked open, but I couldn't see him. I could only see and feel the water moving in the wake of his body. He breathed and went under. The water kept moving. But I couldn't see where he was.

It was a very long five minutes before the drain was clear and I got out of the pool. Gordo hadn't hit me again, but I suffered almost more, waiting for it.

I sat panting on the edge of the pool and cursed him again, softly.

Night had fallen.

We had brought Gordo down from the show pool because he was just getting too big. He weighed around 1,000 pounds now, and like most heavyweights, he was not built for leaping. Whereas Gordo was gigantic and casual, his topdeck replacement, Bayou, was smallish and eager.

On the way down to the pool, while still in the stretcher, the giant guylli had lashed out his tail and sent diver John Patterson on a short, unscheduled flight through the air, smashing him up against one of the heavy-beamed bleacher supports. Curly-haired Patterson had sunk slowly down the pole into a sitting position, a woozy smile on his face, as if he saw small canary birds going tweet, tweet, tweet, like in the old cartoons.

But that was probably an accident, I had hoped, not something done deliberately to harm him.

Gordo had no reason to thank us for what happened to him after that. On his entry into the petting pool, Arnie was waiting. Arnie, the old Prince of Darkness himself. Not intimidated in the least by Gordo's size, Arnie shot right underneath the giant guylli and slammed his tail upward with such astonishing force that half-ton Gordo was knocked sideways clear up out of the water.

Stopping only for food and rest, the two battled for days.

Once, in a heaving surge of strength, Gordo shoved Arnie over the shallow rise of smooth concrete that divided the petting pool into two sides. Arnie did not stay where he had been pushed, of course, but came right back across to hassle Gordo, who was himself quite willing to continue mixing it up. But the surprise maneuver gave us an idea.

A fence was put up. Arnie had the smaller side; Gordo and the two females, Terry and Spray, played in the larger.

Thus it had stayed until Arnie's death. He was gone now, and I could not truthfully say I missed him.

But lately there were signs that formerly happy-go-lucky Gordo was trying to take over Arnie's role.

Was he becoming embittered, made savage by the stress of captivity?

I was sure of it. I was also sure what would happen next. Gordo would become like Arnie, mean and aggressive — but only for a while. Then he would get sick, and his body wouldn't truly resist the sickness because he would have stopped caring about living. When the mind gives up, so does the body, and Gordo would die of some illness that would normally have been no threat to him.

To a dolphin in captivity, boredom is the ultimate danger.

I gathered my gear and got ready to go home. But the more I thought about Gordo, the more upset I got.

I can't, I thought, I can't just sit by and watch Gordo get bored and mean and sick, and maybe die before his time. No.

An idea flashed into my mind. Something small, maybe even stupid, but something I could do, a way to put myself against what was wrong.

It was also the kind of idea that needs to be carried out at once, before the wiser sense of self-preservation prevails.

Quickly, not allowing myself time to think, I dropped my gear: air line, scrub brush, fins, and mask. In weight belt and wetsuit, I hopped over the low wall into Gordo's pool.

The waves of my entry splashed cold against my face.

Then my voice snapped out, and this time I liked the sound of it: quavery, scared, but alive, and not defeated.

"Come on, you old fat thing! *Let's play!*"

I heard the water hiss. I had just time to think I might have made a very serious mistake, and then something like a half-ton submarine knocked me down.

Like being under a mountain falling, I felt rather than saw his giant torso going over, heard the thump of water walls crashing together, filling the hole my body left. Then Gordo turned and was back on me, poking down with his huge snout. But he made no move to hit.

I had no sense of airlessness yet and, strangely, no fear either. I felt somehow as safe as if I were at home in bed, dreaming. A good dream, too! It felt . . . right.

Without conscious direction, my body reacted. I clutched his bulk above me, used the enormous body to pull myself up. Gordo did not flinch away. He only waited. Still.

Like leaning on a desk, I stood. For a moment, that was enough. I could hardly get my breath. My eyes burned from the salted water. But there I was, on my feet, wiping my face till I could see the huge outline of Gordo before me.

A glimmer of moonlight glanced across a ripple by his eyes.

Putting my hands on his beak, I pushed, slow but hard, trying to make him glide backwards, trying to play shove with Gordo as I had with Ernestine and Spock. But he was too strong; he came forward and knocked me down again. Scrambling back up, I gave it another try, this time shoving his beak to the side. With overwhelming eagerness, the giant dolphin pushed back again. This worked much better. Instead of being knocked off my feet, I was merely slid along the bottom. I surged all my ex-weightlifter's strength against his bulk, but, like wrestling a train, the contest was somewhat one-sided. I could try as hard as I wished, but the train retained the advantage.

As we continued, Gordo's eagerness calmed; he seemed to grow more cautious, gaining understanding of my limits. He held his giant's strength in check, so that I was only exhausted, and not injured, by his power.

We played for perhaps a quarter-hour before I had to say, "Good night, that's all I can handle," and crawl out of the tank.

I felt as if my bones had melted. I was so tired I could barely remain vertical on the way across the bridge, past the diver's shack, and, finally, to the showers.

But seldom have I felt more thoroughly contented.

I couldn't solve all the problems myself, but I wasn't helpless; I could do something.

With conscious effort, all oceanarium dolphins' lives can be made more interesting. Playing with Gordo was obviously not much — one small step up from nothing. But it was a step.

*   *   *

Could we treat dolphins in captivity more fairly? If so, how?

The sabbatical arrangement, which I believe marine-mammal expert Dr. Ken Norris was first to propose, is one possibility. In this plan, an animal would be caught, brought to an oceanarium, worked in shows for several years, and then released back to the wild.

There are worries and problems with this; for example, wild dolphins may not accept "tame" dolphins back into their group, and animals hand-fed for years may not be able to hunt well enough to survive without help.

Still, it's an intriguing idea with tremendous potential, and it should be explored.

My own best wish would be for every oceanarium to have a dolphin community tank, as pioneered by Marine-land of Florida, as well as the usual show pool. We take dolphins from the ocean; let us bring the ocean with them, make their new home really livable. A community tank could have fiberglass reefs in it, fish of hardy species, and maybe a turtle or a shark or two. That way, life would have variety, like in the old Marine World reef aquarium tank, which was so crammed with interacting species that it never seemed to be the same tank two days in a row. The dolphins wouldn't grow bored with living: they could enjoy the same thirty- to thirty-five-year life span they do in the wild.

We could measure their contentment by the fact that they would reproduce regularly, just as they did in the old Sea Studios, now Marineland of Florida, where dolphins, sharks, turtles, and fishes lived together.

A multi-species community tank would give the dolphins a natural, stimulating family life. It would be a place for birthing and for retirement. Here dolphin families could play, and visitors could see the panoramic dramas of the ocean.

Doubtless it would be expensive and difficult, as are all great things at first.

But if it were done, the dolphins would reproduce regularly and reliably. We could take new show dolphins from our own tank-raised population.

And never again would we need to take wild dolphins from the sea.

I visited Gordo to wrestle and play as often as I could after that — almost every day. I would either get into the tank and wrestle with him, if the park was closed, or just call him over and grab him by the tail if there were guests. I would drag him back and forth and talk semi–baby talk to him: "Hello, you old fat thing, yes, you are fat, don't you tell me you are not!" — and suchlike happy nonsense.

We had a private signal between us. I would place my hand on the surface of the pool and push it suddenly down. This made a quiet little *thump!* underwater, and Gordo would know it was me. He would leave anybody or anything (except food) and come rushing over to visit. He didn't have good vision in the air, so the signal was perfect for us.

The active tussling appeared to make a difference to him, because the huge Pacific dolphin was calmer with the divers when we had to go into his tank to pull fish off his drain. But there weren't a whole lot of fish to pull anyway, because his appetite came back to normal.

It was just about this time, too, that Gordo's involvement with Project Circe began.

Project Circe was a long-range dolphin research project. It focused not only on human-dolphin communication but on their total intelligence: how they learned, what they remembered, how they communicated with each other.

It was the best thing that could have happened to Gordo.

Dr. Diana Reiss, the leader of the project, had black hair and big eyes and talked about two miles a minute. She plainly loved the creatures she was working with. "It's important that dolphins retain power and control over their environment," she would say, and she believed strongly in the value of a dolphin community tank.

Hardworking and thorough, Diana kept exhaustive records. Her videotapes alone would be a treasure trove of research information for years to come.

But more important for Gordo, the research project was something interesting to do. There were a lot of different parts to the project. One of them was a keyboard that went into the water. Gordo could poke one button for toys, another for a fish, another for a rubdown. The huge Pacific guylli would push that last one over and over, as he purely loved to get his belly scratched.

Gordo never did turn mean.

In fact, years later when I told Diana that Gordo had once seemed on the edge of turning mean, she was astonished. Then she said, "You know, it's funny, but sometimes when I go swimming with him, he comes right up to me and wiggles his head side to side." This was Gordo's "wrestling" movement, which we had worked out together.

Gordo remained what he was by nature: the friendliest dolphin I ever saw, both with people he knew and sometimes with total strangers. He would roll on his back and with his pec fin pat the water invitingly, and even the most determinedly dignified individuals would find themselves leaning over the wall and scratching his big belly. Gordo's chubby charm was irresistible. I cannot imagine anybody meeting him and continuing to think that dolphins were "gangsters of the sea" who should be killed for eating fish.

Gordo's life wasn't perfect. His tank didn't provide the wildlife variety of the living sea. There were no fish there with him, except for the thawed-out ones he ate. Still, he and the two female dolphins named Terry and Spray (later renamed Circe, in honor of the project) did live together for quite a few years in relative contentment in the petting pool.

There were no other dolphin males in the area, which meant Gordo had no competition for his mates' attention.

Until one morning . . .

10

Two Miracles
in Three Days

Terry had been doing what looked very much like sit-ups for several months. She would hang straight up and down in the water, then lean forward and seem to try to touch her head to her tail. Of course she could not do it; dolphin spines are stiffer than ours, not flexible enough for that sort of contortion.

But Terry still did this strange sit-up exercise nearly every day, at first just once a day or so, then more and more often, until the movement could be observed nearly every hour.

Circe did it too.

There was one possible reason for it, but that explanation didn't seem likely to me.

In the past, blood tests had indicated that Terry might

be pregnant, but nothing had happened, so I was skeptical when new park veterinarian Dr. Laurie Gage told me about the most recent test. In the eighteen years of Marine World's existence, there had never been a dolphin baby born here.

Not alive.

Then one morning, Terry began to race around the tank like one of those motorcycles that goes so fast in its circular arena that it can go up on the walls.

Faster and faster Terry swam, and so high that one of the researchers could catch glimpses of something underneath, protruding, like a dark, still flower at the base of her belly.

Round and round she raced, and then she slowed, and stopped, and a little patch of blood appeared where she had been.

I thought about the suction on the drain, and how small, limp things falling would get stuck on it. I thought about Ernestine, and the baby she had almost had.

And then . . . and then . . .

No. It couldn't be. Our eyes must be mistaken, a shadow only, our imagination —

Yes, yes, there it was again!

A miniature Gordo broke the surface in a casual arc, swimming beside its mother, calm, as if it were no miracle at all.

"*Ptoo-hssp!*" Gordo's son (as we would later determine) took his first breath.

Wobbly, yes, and he shivered because he was cold, but he was a baby! A real little baby dolphin, just right there, swimming along, cutest thing you ever saw.

He was four feet long and weighed about a hundred

pounds. His forehead bulged forward, like a little tough guy wearing a cap pushed low over his eyes. His skin was wrinkly; the blubber hadn't thickened yet because the blanketing insulation hadn't been needed in the warmth of the womb.

Now he needed milk, which he would find at one of the two small bulges at the base of Terry's stomach. The presence of the two slits behind which milk nipples lie is one of the ways dolphin sexes can be told apart.

The baby was not very exact as to the location of the faucet, but Momma guided him. When he was close enough, a small black nipple popped out, and nobody had to tell

him what to do next. The hungry newborn wrapped a surprisingly long and flexible tongue around the nipple, encircling it like a wide pink straw. Like all dolphins, the baby had no real lips and therefore could not suck. But that was no problem. Terry just flexed her muscles, and her milk shot into her baby's throat.

His name was Panama. His mother was an Atlantic bottlenose dolphin; his father was from the Pacific: it was perfect for the baby to be named for the canal that links these two oceans of the world sea.

Gordo was naturally curious about the baby and came rushing over to investigate.

But new-mother Terry snapped her jaws at the male, warning him that he was not welcome.

But . . . but . . . !!!

Visibly hurt by her rejection, Gordo went to sulk beside Circe. If Terry didn't want him around, he would stay with Circe.

Except that three days later Circe began to swim rapidly around the tank, as if warming up for a race.

And as if our lives hadn't had enough excitement recently, to Gordo's (and our) astonishment, there was a fifth inhabitant of the tank! Another baby! Also a male, the second newborn was named Delphi, Latin for dolphin. In eighteen years no dolphin babies had been successfully born at Marine World: then, in three days' time, two of them!

But now the situation turned serious.

Dolphin males can be cruel to newborns, sometimes treating them so roughly that the infants die. No one knows why. Perhaps it is nature's way to make the babies afraid of sharks, which are also large and gray and not to be made friends with.

Or maybe it is simply that those dolphins observed hadn't had enough experience with babies.

Apes have this problem sometimes. One zoo-raised mother gorilla had never seen a newborn of her kind before, and when her own arrived she didn't know what to do with it. Grasping her infant's arm between her thumb and forefinger, she pinched just a little — and broke the baby's arm.

For this reason, newborn chimpanzees are often raised by surrogate mothers, humans taking the place of a chimpanzee mother. If a new mother chimp did not know how to take care of her newborn right away, one of the Africa USA folks would nurture the baby so that it would survive.

But this substitute mothering wouldn't work here.

Newborn baby dolphins should not be touched by humans. This was discovered by tragic accident. One park was delighted when a dolphin gave birth. Eager to check the newborn over medically, the humans lowered the water to catch the baby, and as human hands touched the infant, it stopped living — just died instantly. Everyone was horrified. No one really knew why it happened, but possibly the infant was so shocked at being separated from its mother that it just let go its hold on life.

No, whatever happened in the petting pool would have to be up to the dolphins themselves. For us to interfere in any way could mean death to the newborns.

When Gordo saw that there were now *two* of the little creatures in the pool, and nobody he could play with anymore, he threw a fit. For *him* to be ignored? One day he was the star of the place, with two females who plainly adored him, and all the tankside human visitors he wanted, and the research project too. Now Terry and Circe both shunned him, and even the people were fenced off. He'd dropped from stardom to become the outcast of the tank.

Raging, he snapped his giant jaws and flung his enormous body thrashing around the pool, faster and faster, like a submarine making impossibly tight corners.

Waves began to rise. The blue sea rose higher and higher, overlapping the walls, flooding over the edge. We watched in horror, not knowing what to do.

Once a dolphin had been flung out of, or had jumped out of, this very tank. I saw her afterward, her body raked and torn from falling on the decorative lava rock. She had very nearly died from the impact of the fall. I always suspected Arnie had flung her out, but I had no evidence to prove it.

Now I could only watch and worry as the waves swirled higher and higher. The volunteers ran back and forth, arms outstretched as though praying for rain, and it would have been funny if it hadn't been so serious. I went and sat down on the biggest rock, on the far side of the divider. If one of the babies was pitched out here, I figured, I might be able to deflect him from the air back to the pool.

The waves soared so high around the sides of the tank that the water in the middle dwindled to almost nothing, and every so often the center drain sucked air, and you could see the dolphins inside the waves, higher than the walls.

But the mothers raced around the tank, staying always on the outside, their bodies between their infants and the danger. And each baby kept one fin in contact with his mother's stomach and bodysurfed beside her.

It was wonderful. The giant wave could have pitched the dolphins out to virtually certain death, but the mothers kept their babies safe. Now I could understand how dolphin infants could survive a storm, how cetacean mothers, without fingered hands, could still protect their babies: they carried them along wherever they went, the little ones bodysurfing on the ripples that their mother's torso made.

Even before the water was calm, nets were being brought and strung up around the pool to prevent the babies from being pitched out.

Gordo went to a corner of the big side of the tank and

brooded. He was surrounded by family, but in a way he was alone.

I felt sorry for him, but what could be done? We couldn't lower the water and remove him, take him to a place where he could get more attention and be no threat to the newborns. Had we done so, even the lowering of the water to catch the enormous animal would probably have over-stressed the newborns, making them so nervous that they'd die. There was, of course, no question of catching him in deep water!

The mothers appeared to have no time to be sympathetic to a sulking father. He would just have to understand, their attitude seemed to say.

I wanted to explain to them, "Hey, Gordo needs to be a part of this. Let him know he is a father, or there will be nothing but trouble ahead. Get him involved somehow!"

I remember my own daughter's birth, and how incredible it had felt to be inside the delivery room and to hold my child, my Desirée, for the first time. My wife had made me promise to count the baby's toes, and I was trying to do that, but when I actually held my daughter in my hands, she was so beautiful that I started crying and the tears blocked my vision. I kept losing track of how many toes there were and had to start all over again. That was joy unimaginable, like a bolt of lightning striking through the body without harm. Come on, Gordo, understand!

But Gordo did not understand.

And Panama and Delphi, the second son, were always there, always, and they did not go away.

Gordo snapped his jaws at them.

*   *   *

One day Panama, the firstborn, went exploring, on the wrong side of the tank. He zipped across the divider between the two tanks, to the place where Arnie had once lived.

He didn't know that there could be a hidden danger there.

Perhaps because of the smaller amount of water above it, the drain on the small side of the pool sucked harder than the one on the larger side. To an adult the extra suction was no problem, but could an infant be sucked down, and held? I had felt that suction, and it was strong. Larry Ropa and Pete Cobb of the filtration department had foreseen the problem and had turned the suction way down . . . but the dolphins didn't know that.

Gordo watched as Panama swam across the central divider, and his mother screamed, and Panama ignored her.

This time the mother couldn't help. She was afraid of that side, perhaps because of the shallowness of the divider, or the suction, or maybe even the memories of Arnie, who had lived there. Even to protect her child, Terry couldn't make herself cross that line. She whistled a scream, but Panama was having fun exploring that new forbidden side, and he stayed there.

Gordo took command. He roared. There is no better word to describe his violence bark, that single most serious threat an adult dolphin can make.

The baby didn't wait to see what was the matter. He hurtled back to his mother as fast as his little flukes could take him.

Mom was furious and punished her calf in the approved dolphin manner, holding him pinned underwater against the floor for a solid thirty seconds. This helpless feeling makes a definite impression on any freedom-loving dolphin calf.

But after the baby was disciplined, Gordo did something astonishing. He communicated his wishes to the dolphin kid in the clearest and most unmistakable way.

Clumsily, the enormous dolphin lumbered his giant self up onto the divider between the two pools. Gordo didn't like that shallow place. It was dryness, and more: the fear of almost being beached, trapped, experiencing once more the terrible crush of his own weight on land, as he had when captured so many years before. But he went up there any-way, onto the divider, to warn — and thereby to protect — his children.

Awkwardly Gordo turned sideways on the divider, block-ing it with his huge body.

Then he barked and snapped his jaws. He shook his head and smacked his tail and swelled up with indrawn air. In every way he could, he told his little ones, "Stay away from here! Danger!"

When Gordo finally did slide off the divider, he ap-proached the babies again, first one and then the other, and this time the mothers did not interfere.

Gordo looked the babies over from one end to the other, and Circe and Terry seemed to change their minds about him. From then on, the huge male was allowed to help with the work of raising the dolphin babies. He could be involved and interested in his children's lives. Truth to tell, the mothers were doubtless glad to have somebody to share the chores. Gordo naturally couldn't help with the feeding, and there weren't any diapers to change, but he could certainly watch the little ones when a mother needed a break. In the wild, dolphin mothers have "aunties" for this purpose, other females who will help with the babysitting chores.

But in this tank now, both females were busy, and it was a very good thing for everyone when Gordo turned out to be a good father after all.

Epilogue:
One Dolphin Memory

*I*f I had to choose one dolphin memory, just one, but something shining, to warm me as I grow old, it would be this final story.

It happened not long after I first signed on with Marine World.

I was in the dolphin show pool and had been scrubbing algae off the floor for a long time. I was by myself and getting tired. But it was a good, healthy fatigue, the kind that makes you strong and lets you sleep at night. And it brought something else as well: physical tiredness can sometimes increase a person's sensitivity, so that he or she feels things more deeply — as if the minor troubles of the day become too much hassle to bother with and are put aside for later. The mind forgets the past and doesn't worry about the future. For a brief time, we live truly in the present, in the now.

And on this day, in the pure and lovely blue of underwater, I heard an unfamiliar noise: a sort of sweet, warbling whistle, like birdsong. I didn't remember hearing it before. It wasn't the normal clicks and squeaks and buzzes; this was somehow different . . . warmer? inviting?

And then Ernestine was before me, my Ernestine, her body perfect, untouched by marks or scars of any kind. She arched her head and upper back slightly to one side. Like most dolphin species, Ernestine had no real neck (the topmost section of the spine is fused together), and the motion was a little stiff, but still it looked very much like an invitation to play.

I hesitated. Lucky was very much alive then, and he didn't always approve of my getting friendly with Ernestine. On several occasions the dominant dolphin had stopped me when I had spent too much time with her. When he thought she had soared with me too long between the floor and the silver-mirrored surface, *klonk!* Lucky would snap his jaws, and Ernestine would ditch me at once, shaking away from my lightly gripping fingers with one toss of her powerful torso. Lucky would give me "The Look" as his lady friend rejoined him.

So I thought it safer to ignore Ernestine this time, and I did so.

But then a short, thick beak poked me in the elbow. Huh? What? I looked up into the calm and confident eyes of Lucky. Was I being ordered out of the tank? It didn't feel like that. It felt like . . . fun, like an adventure trying to happen, and I wasn't going to let a chance like this pass by.

I opened my fingers and didn't watch the scrub brush fall. Hurriedly I unbuckled my belt and slid off three lead weights. As they clunked to the bottom, I leaped lightly from the floor . . . and flew.

By happy thought I brought my legs together in the kick named after these wondrous fliers of the sea. I held my arms against my sides and dolphin-kicked as one long body instead of separately working arms and legs. I soared, released, swimming up a sunbeam, into the warmth and the light.

Suddenly four dolphins were around me, above, below, touching my shoulders left and right. I felt the warmth of their bodies as they swam, slowly, considerately keeping to a pace my human strength could match. We were five lives together: Ernestine, Lucky, Spock — even Arnie! — and me, four dolphins and a man in the middle, kicking around the tank as naturally as if we had always done it.

I got a grip on two dorsal fins, and they rushed forward, hurtling as fast as speedboats underwater, and all I could see was blue and the white lights racing by and the backs of the dolphins rising and falling, and I was with them.

My body motions felt complete, whole, coordinated — not clumsy as I am on land where I bump into things. No, here, I was graceful!

Ernestine kicked off and I followed, chasing her in play, without the slightest fear of being misunderstood — not on this day.

With all the strength of my body I pulled after her, not swimming with fins alone, but hooking my hands into the blue and tugging, yanking with forearms, triceps, shoulders. Even my back muscles got into the act as I went roaring

through the water, surging, reaching hugely, faster than I'd ever swum before. And just out of reach she glided — my Ernestine! — serenely kicking on her back. However hard I tried, however much I rushed my human swimmer's pace, I could not close the distance between us.

At last my body engine overheated, and, huffing and puffing, I had to stop. Ernestine rejoined me. Her presence was like warm and gentle laughter, with no sting in it, as if she were saying, "Did you really think you could outswim me?"

She offered me her fin. We caught up with the others and soared on, like notes in a song, like happy dancers in a dream.

Never had I experienced such emotions — such peace, and such power. My mind soared free. Nothing seemed impossible. Obstacles existed only for the joy of leaping over them, and the strongest energy of earth was love.

The sea united us, as it does our entire water planet.

We were one blood: the ocean, the dolphins, and me.